Sacred Journeys

SACRED
JOURNEYS

WENDY MURRAY
ZOBA

TYNDALE HOUSE PUBLISHERS, INC
WHEATON, ILLINOIS

Visit Tyndale's exciting Web site at www.tyndale.com

Sacred Journeys

Copyright © 2002 by Wendy Zoba. All rights reserved.

Cover photograph copyright © 2001 by Deborah Jaffe/Stone. All rights reserved.

Title page and part title page photograph © Photodisc.

Designed by Beth Sparkman

Edited by Susan Taylor

Names of people, places, and minor details of events in chapters 5 through 8 have been changed to protect the privacy of those involved.

The story of Mary in chapter 1 first appeared in the December 11, 1995, issue of *Christianity Today* magazine.

Portions of chapter 9, "The Road Less Traveled," are adapted from "The Choice," an article that appeared in the summer 1997 edition of *Marriage Partnership* magazine.

Portions of chapter 10, "Visions," are adapted from "How We Die," an article that appeared in the April 8, 1996, issue of *Christianity Today* magazine.

Unless otherwise indicated, all Scripture quotations are taken from the *Holy Bible,* New Living Translation, copyright © 1996. Used by permission of Tyndale House Publishers, Inc., Wheaton, Illinois 60189. All rights reserved.

Scripture quotations marked NIV are taken from the *Holy Bible,* New International Version®. NIV®. Copyright © 1973, 1978, 1984 by International Bible Society. Used by permission of Zondervan Publishing House. All rights reserved.

Scripture quotations marked RSV are taken from the *Holy Bible,* Revised Standard Version, copyright © 1946, 1952, 1971 by the Division of Christian Education of the National Council of the Churches of Christ in the United States of America, and are used by permission. All rights reserved.

Scripture quotations marked KJV are taken from the *Holy Bible,* King James Version.

Scripture quotations marked "NKJV" are taken from the New King James Version. Copyright © 1979, 1980, 1982 by Thomas Nelson, Inc. Used by permission. All rights reserved.

Library of Congress Cataloging-in-Publication Data

Zoba, Wendy Murray.
    Sacred journeys / Wendy Murray Zoba.
       p. cm.
    Includes bibliographical references.
    ISBN 0-8423-5509-X (pbk.)
    1. Christian life.   2. Family—Religious aspects—Christianity.   I. Title.
BV4515.2 .Z63 2002
248.4—dc21   2001006548

Printed in the United States of America

08   07   06   05   04   03   02
7   6   5   4   3   2   1

To the ones
whose lives
inhabit these pages,
on earth and in heaven.

❋

✵ CONTENTS ✵

ACKNOWLEDGMENTS

I am grateful to many people for enabling me to complete this project. Foremost, I am indebted to my agent and friend, Mickey Maudlin, who captured the vision for this book, found the right publisher, helped me bring abstract notions into concrete expression, and elevated my rambling text with his keen editorial instincts. The good people at Tyndale then brought their expertise to bear and further elevated the project with their excellent oversight. Sue Taylor, my editor, has been right on in her suggestions and conferred them to me with warmth, grace, and a feeling of friendship.

I would also like to acknowledge the many people whose lives and deeds are recounted in these pages. My sisters, Sue Thomas, Carol Harrison, and Nancy Servis, have graciously allowed me to share our story in the chapter titled "Sisters' Reunion." Carol, too, opened her heart by enabling me to tell the story about her dear daughter Kelly, recounted in "Kelly's Gift." My husband, Bob, willingly surrendered his story in "The Road Less Traveled," and my sons Ben and Jon had no qualms about my extravagant display of their Calvinist impulses in the chapter titled "Jesus Freaks." Our friend and Jon's former coach, John Duraski, allowed me to recount the wrenching details of our son's eighth-grade wrestling season of which he was so much a part, as noted in the chapter titled "Coach." I am indebted to my aunt, Sue Bentel Bieniasz, who kindly surrendered to me my grandmother's journals, letters, and poems; and to my mother, Barbara Bentel Murray, who also offered much help in piecing together the early life of my grandmother, as it is depicted in the chapter titled "Eternity Backwards."

Introduction

〜

When my husband and I said farewell to our second son (of three) as he left home for college, there were moments I asked myself why I had had children. Was it worth this much pain? You give them your heart, and then they take it and run. All you've got left is the mess they left in their bedroom.

Are we meant to grow up in the context of these intimate family bonds only to have them ripped and severed? So much can—and does—go wrong in the process of "family life." As a child you may do things that hurt people before you can understand the ramifications of the pain you've caused. And those people may do things that hurt you, and they don't understand that either. You resent them or they resent you, and it takes half your adult life to get over it. Some people never get over it. You battle to shed the skin of your heritage, to find out who you are apart from these people. You come into your own. You find your calling and maybe a husband or a wife. Maybe you have children. That brings with it the chance to start over and impute to these beautiful small people all those things that weren't imputed to you. Or you choose not to impute, as the case may be. If you are a parent, your children look to you with saucer eyes, and you discover a reservoir of love that you never imagined could grow out of a heart like yours. You comb their hair and teach them to say please and help them understand the boundaries. They grow up. Maybe they remember what you've taught them; maybe they don't. Then the process of shedding skin begins all over again. Only this time, you are the skin being shed. Then, maybe you look back and reclaim that heritage—that skin—you once so easily dismissed.

It took me a while to figure out that this was a good thing; that God intended to re-create us, to build and rebuild us out of the raw materials of our past and the possibilities yet to come. He does this through family, people you are covenanted to but whom you don't always understand (and vice versa). These are the people who know you too well (and vice versa) and from whom nothing is hid. Family is God's refining fire, through whom he burns the dross out of us and hammers us into useful tools. It requires dying the many small deaths that come with the process of shedding the old skin and finding the new one.

Through family God shows us his heart. When your children turn away and resist your guiding hand, God himself has gone there before you: "Is not Israel still my son, my darling child? . . . I had to punish him, but I still love him. I long for him and surely will have mercy on him." I understand God's forbearance when I am "putting up" with someone's offense against me. I understand his mercy when others are putting up with me. Familial love demands forbearance and mercy, and the capacity to move beyond human inclination. Through family, God reminds us where we have come from (family is good at that) and pushes us into new possibilities, feeding, renewing, and rescripting our failures. His grace fuels the family system. He grows us through it.

In the chapters that follow, I share ways God has used my family to show himself to me. Through the forging process of my childhood and the challenges of marriage and mother-hood I have shed many skins. I have also been the skin that others have shed. The one constant on both sides of that process has been God pulling me closer to his heart.

These stories highlight moments in the lives of many people who did not ask or expect to be born into the family of a writer. I am not trying to tell their stories. They all have stories that are their own. The events in these pages make up my story, parts of which they have shared. Some relate moments of hilarity—humor being one of God's ironic gifts—and others recount passages of darkness. Jesus' follow-ers encountered many events during their sojourn with him, and as the Gospel narratives attest, they did not remember them uniformly. They remembered the good and the painful moments differently while the overall witness was cohesive and consistent.

Those whose lives have intersected with mine may not remember these moments the way that I have recounted them. It is not their fault that they were born in relationship to me. As a writer I am by nature an observer, and so an interpreter of the world around me. Where I may have gotten the story wrong, I assume responsibility for it.

When I think about why I have written down these things, I keep hearing the words of Mary, the mother of Jesus, which is why I have opened the book with her story. When Mary recognized the marvelous and haunting implications of her son's destiny, Luke recounted at two different points, "She treasured these things in her heart." At some point, however, when the time was right, she conveyed them to Luke, who then wrote them down for you and me. Luke was not interested in dishing the dirt on Mary and Jesus. He had a love story to tell, bigger and more wonderful than the gritty details of Mary's everyday life. That is the magic of the way God works: He uses the mundane moments in the muck of real life to reveal his extravagant love. He uses family. So, while the following pages relate events and circumstances connected to my life, to my story, it is also your story, every-one's story. That is because these narratives are, like the Gospels, a story about God.

PART ONE

WATER TO WINE

# 1 *A Sword through Her Soul*

If anyone faced a complicated family dynamic, it was Jesus'
Jewish mother, Mary, whose firstborn was the "begotten one
of God." Things were complicated even before the child was
born, when the terms were set and Mary, dutifully, complied.
"Yes," she said, "I am the Lord's servant. Yes, may everything
you have said come true." It is easy to say such things during
moments of heavenly revelation or, in her case, visitation. We
would all be "the Lord's servants," I daresay, when looking
upon the face of a visiting angel. We would all, like Mary,
agree to the plan.

The test comes, however, when "the plan" intersects with
real life. For Mary, it meant sticking with the plan despite
maternal instincts that contradicted it. Her arena of testing
came in her role as a mother. But the role we find ourselves
in—when it comes to the plan and the test—is beside the
point. We may be single or married, parent or childless,
young or old. The role doesn't matter. The point is the test

and keeping with the plan when circumstances and instincts militate against doing so.

Mary can help us, not because she was a good mother struggling with the changing nature of her bond with her son, but because in the arena of testing she wrestled with real-life emotions in the face of God's mysterious orchestration. Even the "big players" in God's story—our so-called Bible heroes—empowered by angelic visitations and other miraculous interventions, carried pain, weakness, and sorrow upon their breasts. Sometimes our "heroes" weren't sure if they even saw God in the picture.

That is why Mary's struggle introduces the other struggles in this book. Her struggles were as particular to her as mine are to me—and yours are to you. But hers, and mine, and yours point to something greater. That is, God uses real people in the hard places of real life to work out his plan, often sown in tears and struggle and human failing. It is why God, not Mary or other "big players," is the hero of the Bible.

So I return to Mary's story, a story about a mother whose son, she could rightly say, was "special." But special or not, he was her firstborn son, and that carried with it all the longing and apprehension that is the hallmark of parenthood.

Imagine her thoughts when bringing her six-week-old infant to the temple in Jerusalem to "present him to the Lord" as Jewish law required.* The temple courtyard had to have smelled, with animals wandering around, all that dirt

---

*References for Scripture quotations and sources for other material referenced in this book are located in the sources section in the back of the book.

and sewage. Strangers carrying birds in cages or dragging along goats or sheep came and went, sacrificing this or consecrating that. What first-time parents wouldn't feel overwhelmed?

If all the braying, snorting, and howling of animals on the temple grounds were not enough, a strange old man approached Joseph and Mary and "took the child in his arms." At this point Mary may have been thinking, *Has he washed his hands?* His name was Simeon, and he said strange things: "I have seen the Savior you have given to all people. He is a light to reveal God to the nations, and he is the glory of your people Israel!"

How could he know such things?

He turned to Mary and looked at her with sad eyes. "And a sword will pierce your very soul."

That wasn't the impression Mary had gotten the day the angel Gabriel appeared to her. Gabriel had said, "Don't be frightened, Mary, . . . for God has decided to bless you! You will become pregnant and have a son, and you are to name him Jesus. He will be very great and will be called the Son of the Most High." *What could this ridiculous old man Simeon be thinking?*

One might naturally assume that Simeon was referring to the anguish Mary experienced when she watched her son die. She remained with him throughout his ordeal, standing beneath his cross until he breathed his last. There could be no darker moment for any mother. Yet my own reading of the Gospels convinces me that the "sword" that pierced Mary's soul did so many times before that moment. Such piercings are the movements of faith and the work of God's grace, though at the time they don't feel that way, and they didn't feel that way to Mary. Even she could not escape hard lessons about conforming her inclinations to the greater purpose of God's plan. Often those lessons were for her (and are for us) tangled in a web of fragile and often conflicting emotions. Yet for all the moments of heartache she surely endured, there still must have also been countless times when she beamed with pride over her firstborn son and wanted to shout, "That's my boy!" Mary was, as I've said, a Jewish mother.

❊ ❊ ❊

I have had such moments of pride with my three sons over the years, and this has helped me understand Mary. One moment that stands out occurred when we lived in Honduras several years ago. Jon, our youngest, played right field for the Little League baseball team called the *Promesas* (Spanish for "Promises"). The *Promesas,* in a word, stunk. They had not won a game all season. During this particular game, we were losing 12 to 7 in the bottom of the eighth.

Jon stepped up to the plate. The opposing team had brought in a new pitcher. He struck out the first two *Promesa* batters without breaking a sweat. But it didn't take long before he started getting overconfident. Soon he was throwing balls. And just like that, the bases were loaded with walked *Promesa* batters.

Our team was down by five runs. A home run would erase four and make it, for once, a real game. That's when Jon came up to bat. For all the chatter and mayhem coming from the stands, you would have thought that the Honduran democracy stood or fell on what the boy did at the plate.

His coaches were yelling frantic instructions: *"¡Chóquela, Juan! ¡Cuídala!"* ("Choke up, Jon! Watch it now!") Honduran moms won all the prizes for enthusiasm, twirling noisemakers, whistling, jumping up and down, stomping their feet (some in high heels). The stadium crowd was on their feet. Jon was still only learning Spanish, but he got the point. Even so, he seemed tentative. This was detectable in subtle movements that only a mother could pick up. He stood in the batter's circle, waiting to bat, and sliced the bat halfheartedly. He jostled his helmet and fiddled with his batting gloves. He tapped his shoe with the bat. Then it was his turn to step into the batter's box.

Making my way down the bleachers, I pressed against the chain-link fence behind the batter's box. I knew better than to try to get Jon to look at me. I didn't need his personal acknowledgment. I just wanted him to hear my voice.

"Don't back off this guy, Jon. He's getting tired. He's wild. Meet the pitch. Keep your eye on it."

He scraped home plate with his shoe, cocked his head, adjusted his helmet, and crouched, elbows up, in the batting position. *"¡Juan! ¡Juan! ¡Juan!"* The crowd was roaring behind him.

"You can do it, Jon!" I yelled to him.

Don't you know that boy made contact the very first pitch—a blooper down the middle, between second and third. Two base runners scored, and Jon lost his batting helmet pedaling

7

around the bases. He settled at second, and the crowd had gone wild. I couldn't even yell, "That's my boy!" because of the lump in my throat. Safe at second base, he pulled off his batting gloves, shoved them in his pocket, and put his hands on his knees. He threw me a look, and that was my moment. I felt like the Queen of All Mothers. That was *my boy*. *I* was his mom. Apart from the bat's meeting the ball, in that moment that was the only connection that mattered.

Mary must have had many such queen-motherish moments. Her son "grew . . . in height and in wisdom, and he was loved by God and by all who knew him." Yet at the same time, contrary to my experience at the ball game, Mary's son did not always pass her a knowing look that warmed her heart at certain defining moments. That troubled me when I read these narratives. At times Jesus seemed insensitive, if not rude, to his mother. Imagine the wonder and pride that welled up in the young virgin after Gabriel's visit. She was to give birth to the only Son of God! "I rejoice in God my Savior! . . . Now generation after generation will call me blessed."

But that might have been the last time we see Mary unequivocally happy. That transcendent moment quickly became overshadowed by a steady stream of heartwrenching moments that tested Mary's trust in the plan. The first would be the unenviable task of telling her fiancé, Joseph, that she was pregnant. (Joseph took it well, considering.) The next would be the hard journey on an ass, nine months pregnant, cross country, only—third—to end up giving birth in a cave in the company of goats and sheep. I would wager these inconveniences evaporated once she held the little one in her arms and suckled him at her breast—her very own son, the glorious creature she had pushed through her loins! But this wondrous event began a journey of faith that exacted many more piercings of Mary's soul.

There was the time, for example, when Mary and Joseph traveled to Jerusalem with their prepubescent boy to celebrate the Jewish festival of Passover. At the end of the festival, they left for home, assuming that Jesus was with friends among their fellow travelers. But failing to find him among their relatives after the first day of travel, they realized they had left their young boy behind in Jerusalem (the big city!) and undertook a desperate search that lasted for three days.

I can relate to the desperation Mary and Joseph must have felt as they searched for Jesus. For a brief, bone-chilling interlude sixteen years ago we lost our two-year-old son on the Mall in Washington, D.C. One minute he was toddling at our feet, and the next he was nowhere to be seen. In that single moment I was overrun with terror, panic, and utter helplessness until we found him, thankfully, climbing a fence several yards away. (Sons climbing things is a cross mothers of sons must bear.) By that point my pulse rate had dropped, my skin waxed ashen, and my knees felt ready to give way.

Jesus' parents carried such terror for three days—*three days*. Mary couldn't have slept much, which wouldn't have helped her mood. I have sometimes wondered if Mary entertained thoughts like I do when I am watching a suspense film that stars Robert DeNiro—you know he won't die. He can't die. He's the star. He's Robert DeNiro! That eases the suspense for me. Maybe, given the optimistic account received from Gabriel, Mary thought, *Okay, he's lost, but it's not supposed to end this way. He's the Messiah. We'll find him.*

Indeed, they found him, surrounded by religious leaders, chatting casually in the temple. Mary was understandably miffed. "Son! . . . Why have you done this to us? Your father and I have been frantic, searching for you everywhere." Who could blame her? She hadn't slept for two nights and had been searching frantically for days. And when they finally found him, did he run to their waiting arms, expressing relief and affection? To the contrary, he was nonchalant. Had he not been the Messiah, one might have thought him an upstart in need of an attitude adjustment. Worse, the twelve-year-old turned the rebuke of the parents back upon them. He responded by saying two things: First, he said, they should have known where he would be ("Why did you need to search?"); and second, God—not Joseph—was his father ("You should have known that I would be in my Father's house.") They should have known that, too.

Despite the remonstrance, when it was said and done, Jesus returned with his parents to Nazareth and "was obedient to them."

I have often wondered what the day was like for Mary when, as an adult, Jesus heard the call of John the Baptist. By this time Joseph had died, and Jesus had assumed the role of carpenter in his father's shop. In keeping with the law, he would also have taken the mantle of leadership in the family. But the day came when "the call" summoned him. As preacher and seminary professor Fred Craddock describes it,

"Jesus untied the apron strings, lifted the carpenter's apron over his head, put it on the bench and left the shop."

Did he say good-bye to his mother? Did he kiss her on the cheek? *What will you do about dinner?* Or did he depart without a word, leaving Mary to find the shop empty, the apron on the bench?

Maybe Mary thought of Joseph, standing there alone in the empty workshop. His ghost had been overtaken by the scraping and pounding of her firstborn son. Now he was gone, too. *Why do we have children? Is it worth this much pain? You give them your heart, and then they take it and run. All you've got left is the apron on the bench.*

Perhaps, in such a moment, she'd summon the memory of the visit from the angel Gabriel. *I knew this day would come,* she might hear herself say, while in her heart of hearts she hoped maybe it would have worked out differently. After all, so much time had passed since the angel appeared. Maybe God would forget the hard part of the plan.

But God didn't forget. His plan was on track and moving forward. *And a sword will pierce your own soul, too.*

Maybe Mary took heart when she realized that although Jesus no longer lived in the house, she could see him fre-quently. She could remain in his close circle of associates. Maybe that's why she went boldly to him at the wedding in Cana to tell him the wine had run out. Maybe she was tugging at his elbow when she alerted him, "They have no more wine."

He did not say, "Sure thing, Ma. I'll get right on it." In fact, he seemed irked. Some translations record that he called his mother "woman"—not derisively, like "Hey, lady!" but not in a sense that evoked the intimate bond between a mother and son either. His response was curt: "How does that concern you and me?" or "What is there between you and me?" He was redefining the boundaries of this relationship.

Then he added a second rebuke to his mother: "My time has not yet come." Maybe Mary was pressuring him—*Begin already! Get on with your messianic appointment.* After all, he had left the carpenter's shop to do *something.* Or maybe she went to him out of habit. He was the oldest. Aren't they the most responsible? He had always been the one who fixed things.

In the end he answered his mother's request, but only after setting out the terms. He made clear that whatever "glory" he would exhibit in this moment was not derived by her promptings. Their relationship had changed. He might as well have said, "When are you going to stop calling me your son?"

But I'm your mother! A mother can't just stop calling a son a son. Even in the prophets the Lord God himself said, "Can a mother forget her nursing child? Can she feel no love for a child she has borne?"

Mary came to him another time when Jesus was looking overworked. He had gained a groundswell of popularity as a teacher and had become known as one who possesses "unusual" powers. Crowds swarmed around him, touching him and clamoring requests. He was pressed on every side with constant demands for his time and attention. *What kind of mother would I be not to intervene?*

Jesus and his followers sought respite in a home, probably Peter's. But even that was soon overrun with curiosity seekers. The hubbub was so frenzied that "he and his disciples couldn't even find time to eat."

He'll starve. He needs oxygen. The lack of air is affecting his mind. So Mary and the brothers undertook an "intervention." *It's for his own good. He's out of his mind,* they thought. The family did what families do. They rallied around and tried to take him home with them.

When Jesus finally realized his mother and brothers were outside looking for him, did he interrupt his conversation, excuse himself, and make his way out to see them? Did he seek to reassure them? No. In fact, he challenged the very notion of family relationships: "Who is my mother? Who are my brothers?"

The terms of the bond had changed. As far as he was concerned, his family was no longer defined by blood. His family was "anyone who does God's will."

What else could Mary have done? All the angelic revelations and prophetic confirmations in the world did not change the fact that he was still her son.

❊ ❊ ❊

Some time later the people of Jerusalem hailed her son as he entered the city gates riding on a donkey and looking like a king. What an exciting day. "Who is this?" some may have queried.

Mary did not shout, "That's my boy!" A mother knows her son's face. Mary saw that her son's was like flint. Tears streamed down his cheeks. She knew they did not spring from the palms, the "hosannas," and the effervescence of the moment.

The authorities seized her son a week later, and all the disciples fled. Maybe one of them—probably John—went to Mary. She would have been able to tell by the look on his face that the time had come. And so, she went to find her son, to be with him in those final hours. Maybe Mary was numbered among the "great crowds [that] trailed along behind, including many grief-stricken women," as he was making his way to Golgotha, staggering under the weight of the beam.

Can't somebody help him?

Maybe a mother's cries moved the heart of a guard that day when he seized Simon of Cyrene and "forced [him] to follow Jesus and carry his cross."

The next picture we have is of Mary crumpled at her son's bleeding feet. Where else would she be? She used to check him for fevers. She bandaged his cut fingers and washed his cloak. *Curse that man Simeon in the temple! If I never hear another prophecy again, it will be too soon!* And now a heap of tears and wails sitting at the foot of her son's cross is all that remains of a loving mother's pierced soul.

Why did the angel call me favored? Where is the favor in this?

"Dear woman." She would look up and meet the eyes of her dying son, who was trying to speak between gasps for air. "Here is your son." He would turn his head slightly and look at John, the disciple who had brought her. "Here is your mother."

Mother.

Frantic instructions from the crowd was all my boy could hear. "Save yourself! If you are truly king, come down from that cross!" He couldn't speak. It was all he could do to breathe. I didn't need him to acknowledge me. I just wanted him to hear my voice. My son looked at me—and I couldn't utter a word because of the lump in my throat.

He was my boy. I was his mother. No other connection mattered.

Did Mary linger in the carpenter shop the day her son left? Did she pick up the apron from the bench and hang it on the peg? Did she start dinner? Was she confounded by the rebuke at Cana? Or when Jesus asked amid the throng at Peter's house, "Who is my mother?" Such questions and affliction are part of dying the small deaths that precede living new life. Even the handmaiden of the Lord had to be made new. As a mother, Mary needed to understand why her beloved son would treat her that way. He understood that. But he also understood that as a struggling human being, she needed the Savior more. And how could she have found her Savior without first letting go of her son?

2 *Sisters' Reunion*

"No suit."

"Excuse me?" my sister Nancy said.

The small Asian woman wagged her finger and repeated in broken English, "No suit."

Nancy turned and looked at the three other sisters standing behind her. We were wrapped in towels, wearing bathing suits, waiting behind a privacy screen for our turn in the mud bath. Nancy, the youngest sister, had invited us to her home in northern California for a "sisters' reunion." It was February, and the three other sisters, myself among them, had each descended from our respective points east: Sue, the oldest, from our native Ohio. I, number two, from New Jersey. Carol, sister number three, from North Carolina.

"Did she say, 'No suit'?" I whispered to Sue.

Sue was laughing. "I think so."

The small woman was leading my now naked sister

Nancy to the edge of a trough of steaming black ash. Nancy looked back plaintively. She deserved to go first; she got us into this.

She eased her body into the mud and lay down flat in the trough, fully exposed from head to toe. The Asian woman knelt at the foot of the trough, touched her palms together, and bowed her head. She looked as if she were praying. The woman rose and began heaping double handfuls of mud onto my sister's body, beginning at the bikini line. Next she covered Nancy's thighs and then her shoulders. The Asian woman saved the breasts for last.

We groaned.

Carol was next. She threw Sue and me a helpless look and went forth into the mud. Sue and I had no choice but to remove our bathing suits and do our time, each of us lying in the vat while the Asian woman raised her palms and bowed her head. We all felt like sacrifices on the altar of the god of the black slime.

It got easier. The eucalyptus bath followed the vat time. They gave us cucumber water to sip—just the thing—and the four of us bantered about in the bath, expressing shock and hilarity at the vat scenario and mapping out the upcoming phases. The sauna and blanket wrap were yet to come, and we all anticipated our ultimate destiny: the massage tables. Here a fundamental difference arose between the sisters.

"I can't have the guy," I said.

Carol concurred. "No way."

Our older sister Sue said in her older sister voice, "Relax, Wendy, it's only a massage."

"I don't want some strange guy rubbing my body. I'm sorry. It's too weird," I said.

Nancy, playing the diplomat, interjected, "Just tell them you would prefer a masseuse. They won't care."

By the end of the sauna we were flushed and puffy lipped. I could feel my blood-sugar level dropping. The blanket wrap helped. This was the cool-down phase. We lay in separate cubicles, tucked, arms and all, inside cool blankets, like newborn babes fresh out of the womb. It got complicated when the cucumbers on my eyes slid askew. I had never had cucumbers on my eyes before, and it felt good, though, admittedly, I would have preferred to eat them. Harp music played in the background, which dispelled some of my encroaching anxiety over whether or not I would get the guy. Then I heard a male voice.

"Wendy?"

In one lurching gesture I twisted my head, wrenched my neck, and bobbled the cucumbers from my eyes, which forced me to free my arms, up till now held captive by the blanket, and, well, Houdini would have been appalled. The masseur peered down at me with raised pointy eyebrows and an impish grin. I thought women's bodies probably didn't charge him up. Regardless, I ventured boldly, "Would it be all right if I had the woman? Nothing personal."

He tilted his head.

"*Ma*ybe," he said. He turned on a heel and pulled the curtain as he left.

❋ ❋ ❋

We are four girls born in the last five and a half years of the 1950s. Sue came first. I arrived twenty-seven months later. Carol came fifteen months after me, and Nancy, twenty-four months after her. Susie. Wendy. Carol. Nancy. My father grew up in a family of all boys, so I think he was in shock. As sisters, we each carved a niche as respective members of the all-female Murray brood. You could envision "the Murray girls" this way: Sue always got straight A's. She was the smart one. Nancy, the tallest and most sultry—and the only natural blonde, like Billie Jo on *Petticoat Junction*—was the pretty one. Carol *enjoyed* grocery shopping with our mother. We called her Susie Homemaker. She was the good one. In due course you'll come to understand why I was the bad one.

When you grow up one of four girls, two things happen: The first is, you get a lot of attention, especially when your mother dresses all of you up in the same outfits. The second is, you get "lost." It takes you half your lifetime to figure out who you are outside of the foursome.

At the same time, our membership in this foursome, such as we were, pulled us through many hard years. When I think about how we sipped cucumber water and tried to clean mud from fingernails and other crevices at the spa—how far we've come from where we used to be—I can measure our destinies only in improbabilities. Our childhood had been covered by the dark shroud of our father's alcoholism, though it took us into our adulthood to see it for what it was. I have also come to see that at the moment when we were powerless to help ourselves, a surprising intervention changed everything. Had our lives finished the course on the trajectory set by our earthly circumstances, we would not have met at the spa that February. We wouldn't have been who or where we are today. We would have been someplace else.

❋ ❋ ❋

Not too long ago my sister Carol gave all the siblings a video-cassette labeled *The Murrays' Greatest Hits*. It included footage from our childhood taken from those silent "home movies" people used to take with bulky cameras and blinding spotlights. Beginning in 1961 and ending in 1969, it is not something anyone would sit down and watch in one sitting. In fact, it is not footage anyone outside the sisters and my mother would want to watch at all. Even my brother, who was born when our ages had all reached double digits, became bored watching it. He doesn't appear until its final moments.

Still, upon receiving it, I gathered my sons around me, popped it in, and highlighted Mommy on the tricycle or Mommy opening Christmas presents at the age of four, or five, or six. The boys laughed once or twice, quickly lost interest, and walked away.

I couldn't walk away. This was my world in washed-out color. This world gave birth to a destiny. There are my grandmother and grandfather, Mema and Pepa, now dead. Women in cotton dresses and horn-rimmed glasses. Men in crew cuts, wearing plaid shorts and loafers and smoking ciga-rettes. Little girls with shiny hair, sitting at a picnic table, sipping milk from a carton with a straw, and waving to the camera. Our mother, slender, with short dark hair. She smiled a lot, and she smoked. Our father, in his black-rimmed glasses, is wearing a cotton shirt with a breast pocket where he keeps his cigarettes. We are in the backyard swimming pool at the Lyndhurst house. Four little girls in ruffled bathing suits, jumping up and down, splashing and being splashed. My aunt and uncle visit. They are carrying beer and holding cigarettes between their fingers. These are some of the ghosts that made up my and my sisters' lives.

Christmas morning 1961. Four little girls in matching red pajamas walk into the living room and pull their stockings from the hooks.

January 1963. I am wearing a party dress with puffy sleeves and a green sash around my waist. My mother stands next to me and lowers the cake. I blow out seven candles. Nancy wants to help me blow, but I don't allow her. It takes me five tries.

Christmas 1963. Dad wipes tired eyes and holds a cigarette. Then he sees the camera and smiles. His face is chubby. There are bags under our mother's eyes.

Easter 1964. Four girls in stiff spring coats, Easter hats, and shiny shoes are on the brick walk out front. "Walk forward," they are told. Carol comes first in her pink coat, then Nancy in her blue one, I in red, and Sue in black.

Christmas 1965. Four girls in polka-dot nightgowns come down the stairs. But something is wrong. Our father is not there. Sue hugs our mother. We are standing around the Christmas tree. Carol jumps up and down. Nancy jumps too.

Christmas 1967. Four girls are wearing fishnet stockings.

They are taller, lankier. They toss their hair back with nods of the head. They slither down the stairs.

1968. Four girls are standing by a thundering waterfall. The wind is pushing them; the water is pelting them. They are not in order. They are not looking at the camera. They are looking at the waterfall, trying to get closer. But they can't.

❀ ❀ ❀

Now that I am grown, I can watch *The Murrays' Greatest Hits* and see forces that shaped the childhood of the sisters. The drinking in our household hadn't become disastrous yet, but it was a regular feature, and the signals were there. The tired puffy eyes. The dark circles. That one Christmas without my father.

My father lost his left eye at the age of four when a bully hit him with a stick and poked it out. He struggled through his childhood because of his handicap, and the bullies made fun of him. Still, he earned the rank of Eagle Scout and was valedictorian of his high school class. He won a full scholarship to Dickinson Law School in Philadelphia, but his mother didn't want him to take it because she said he didn't have the right clothes. So he went to the army instead and then attended Antioch College in Yellow Springs, Ohio, where he met my mother. That is where the first three sisters were born.

We lived in Lyndhurst, Ohio, for the first few years of our childhood. My father had a vision for how to make rubber compounds that held up under intense heat, and he left his job to start his own business in the basement of the house.

Our neighbors, Beau and Ruth, had children our ages, Alan and Lynn. (Alan and I were best friends and were going to be married.) Beau, the engineer, joined my father, the chemist, in launching the new business. Our two families might as well have shared the same house, for all the running back and forth we did. At some point I noticed that Beau and Ruth didn't drink Jim Beam. They drank Cola-Cola out of the glass bottles. I wondered why they didn't drink Jim Beam. I thought everybody drank Jim Beam. I was five when I asked my father for a sip. It went down cold and hot at the same time.

Jim Beam Kentucky Bourbon became a part of our daily life, like a lost relative who moves in and takes over. Both my parents drank it, but my father drank to excess. It became standard procedure at family functions, like weddings, for him to be the first at the bar, pouring drinks for everyone. Then he would be the first to fall down drunk and collapse in a heap. My mother would tell us girls to throw cold water on our faces to reduce the swelling in our eyes from our sobbing. I hated family functions.

These kinds of moments persisted and eventually increased. Mercifully for us, my father left most of his drinking for the evening, when we sisters could be hiding in our rooms. He would nap on the couch in the living room for a while, saving his hard drinking for late at night. I didn't want to hear the sounds coming from downstairs when the fighting started. I hid under the bed sheets and kept the TV going.

The business my father started grew and thrived. He eventually bought a building to house his new company. The business soon outgrew it, and then he bought another, larger, building. In 1962 we left Lyndhurst and moved to Chagrin Falls, Ohio, home of Tim Conway. It was an idyllic hometown, with natural waterfalls at its center, Dink's Restaurant, and an Isaly's ice-cream shop on Main Street. On one level the Murrays lived in the best of all possible worlds. The business was succeeding. We lived in a spacious home with an in-ground pool. Chagrin Falls was the kind of town people visited on Sunday afternoons to buy popcorn at the Popcorn Shop and feed the ducks and visit the falls.

At its peak, my father's company employed about two hundred people. But his successes were not without heart-aches. One year some of my father's closest friends, college friends whom he had taken on to work in his new company, took the recipes for his special patented rubber compounds and started their own competing company. Another time the labor union camped out in the parking lot, stirring up his nonunion workers and mobilizing a strike. Our phones were tapped during that time, and my father received death threats. The callers told him they were going to blow up his company if he didn't unionize. Our family took a trip to Florida that year, but Dad didn't go. He stayed at his factory day and night, sleeping on the couch in his office and eating dinners out of the vending machines. If they were going to blow up his company, they would have to blow him up with it.

From our side of it, we didn't see all these forces that exacerbated my father's need to drink. We saw only their effects. Life in an alcoholic family is full of distractions. There is no family center, no reading corner. Our lives were mop-up operations, reactions to hostile forces. Our actions and imaginings arose from the desire to be *someplace else*. We avoided the quiet. We had a TV in every room and kept as many going as we could, even if no one was watching. Television became my world. I became a spy, like Napoleon Solo and Illya Kuryakin on *The Man from U.N.C.L.E.* I became Dream Girl, the beauty contestant. I was one of the Lennon Sisters singing "Hukilau" on the *Lawrence Welk Show*. I was "lost in space" with Will Robinson, the robot, and Dr. Smith. Billie Jo, Bobbie Jo, and Betty Jo were three sisters on *Petticoat Junction*—the pretty one, the smart one, and the good one. They didn't have a bad sister. I didn't like *Petticoat Junction*.

My mother talked to us about my father's alcoholism only one time that I can remember. She said my father could never stop drinking. The last time he had tried, she said, he ended up in the Cleveland Clinic's psychiatric ward. That was the year he missed Christmas, in 1965. My mother spared us those details. I read in my grandmother's journals later, as an adult, that my father had undergone nine electroconvulsive therapy treatments during his stay in the clinic. Back then they were known as shock treatments. He was in the hospital for many months. He painted oils and made Christmas ornaments out of shells and shiny beads. Sometimes he came home on weekends.

Four sisters faced these nightmares together. And separately.

One night when I was in high school, our parents' fighting in the hallway roused us. Sue called the neighbor, who came and took the sisters for the night. The next day, when we returned, my father was sitting on the couch in our living room with suitcases packed. I didn't know which parent was leaving.

"Are you leaving?" I asked.

My father looked at me. "Do you want me to leave?"

The truth was, it hadn't upset me to see the suitcases. I wanted this to end. If ending it meant one of my parents had to leave, then that's what it meant.

My father wore an eye patch, and when I was growing up, I honestly never noticed it. When I encounter another person wearing an eye patch, I notice it right away. But I never saw my father's. It was just who he was. When he asked, "Do you want me to leave?" I looked at my father, and for the first time I saw his eye patch. Tears were falling down his cheek— one cheek, from his one eye. That's when I saw that he had only one eye to channel all those tears.

"No," I said, and I went to him and hugged him.

"I don't want to leave," he said.

※ ※ ※

During my father's sober moments he taught us to celebrate our Irish heritage, the Murrays having emigrated to America from Northern Ireland. One year for Easter he gave us each a glass egg with green clovers painted on it and one hidden four-leaf clover. When we opened the boxes and pulled out the eggs, holding them up to the light and looking for the hidden four-leaf clover, he said, "It's so you'll never forget you're Irish." Another time, when we were eating lunch in a restaurant, my father (for reasons I still don't understand) said with pride, "Carol and Sue are true Irish." At the time, it shattered me. I thought that meant you had to be either smart or good to be true Irish. Being pretty like Nancy and stubborn like me didn't count.

I was not true Irish. My own stubborn and rebellious nature was becoming evident. When we played army, I had to be the general, or I would quit. When we wrapped our swim towels around our waists to do the hula, I was the one who made up the arm motions. I cheated at Parcheesi. In the summer of '64 four girls in bathing suits walked to the pool: I was the only sister to wear a two-piece. I knew the green rocks in the stream were the slippery ones, but I told my sister, "Be sure to walk *only* on the green rocks—or else you'll fall down." I reached a point where I refused to wear the frilly dresses, stiff coats, and shiny shoes. I traded them in for bell-bottoms, halter tops, and hot pants, and I didn't care what anybody, including my sisters, thought. I was the bad sister, the troubled sister.

Then, as if abnormally born, I, of all people, became "born again." I was sitting on my bed, one minute crying because of the hopelessness of our situation and the next minute laughing. The only conscious thought I had in that moment was Jesus Christ. There's no other way to say it. I didn't have a Bible, so I looked him up in the *World Book Encyclopedia*. I didn't "ask him into my heart." He came in unannounced and uninvited when I was sixteen, in February 1972.

In March, a month after my conversion, we took a family trip to Rome. We visited all the typical sites, the Coliseum, the Roman Forum, St. Paul's Outside the Walls. But it was our visit to St. Peter's Basilica that made an impression on my father. Next to what is believed to be Peter's grave, at the apex of the basilica, is a marble statue of Peter. The carved toes on his feet are worn smooth from pilgrims who have passed by and touched his feet. Next to the statue is an oil painting depicting Peter's death by crucifixion, upside down. My father couldn't take his eyes off that painting. He touched Peter's feet.

Two weeks later, in early April, my mother told me Dad had quit drinking. I had heard that before and remained unfazed, but time proved it true. My father *had* changed. He wasn't drinking, and a new friend, his sponsor from Alcoholics Anonymous, was calling and visiting him. This kind man, whom I never knew, took my father to meetings several nights a week and called him every day. I asked Dad about him one time, and he said, "We're both a couple of drunks trying to keep each other out of the gutter."

My father was delivered from alcoholism within weeks of my unsolicited conversion. He didn't suffer any psychotic episodes and never touched another drink. My father had been dead before, but now he was alive.

That changed the destiny of four little girls.

❄ ❄ ❄

New Testament scholar N. T. Wright describes Jesus' rescue of this world this way: "Jesus was called to throw himself on the wheel of world history, so that, even though it crushed him, it might start to turn in the opposite direction." That is how I see Jesus' rescue of my family. That day as I sat on my bed, he entered my life—not that I had done anything to merit it—and that started to turn the wheel in the opposite direction. Good things began to happen. Other sisters found Christ, or he found them. The former colleagues who had stolen my father's rubber compounds and left his business to compete with him, failed. They asked my father for forgiveness. He forgave them. He gave them jobs. The labor union and my father reached an agreement to let the employees decide whether or not to unionize. They took a company vote, and the workers voted the union down. They trusted my father to take care of them, and he did.

When Dad sold the company later in his life, he could have walked away with millions of dollars. He took a fraction instead, remitting most of the assets back to the workers themselves as part of his employee stock-ownership plan.

My father did not rest in his retirement. He was an inquisitive man and undertook an investigative study of his roots. He learned that his forebears had, indeed, emigrated from Ireland, but they were not Irish. The Murrays are Ulster Scots—Scots who had settled in Ulster, Ireland, under Cromwell in the 1500s. They migrated to America and settled in Pennsylvania, where my father grew up. With newfound exuberance he embraced our Scottish heritage. He made each of the sisters and our brother wooden replicas of the Murray crest. He gave the sons-in-law neckties made from the Murray plaid, representing our clan. And my father agreed that, in all my stubbornness and rebelliousness, I am a true Scot.

❋ ❋ ❋

Four girls, relaxed and exfoliated, sit in a restaurant in
northern California, reflecting on our day at the spa. Sue
and Nancy got the guy for their massage; they were okay with
that. We laugh about the little woman who seemed to be
praying over our naked bodies on that vat of black ash, and
in a way, that picture reminds us of our young lives—helpless,
laid out on an altar not of our choosing, with someone
(probably our grandmothers) lifting palms and praying over
us. Those prayers changed everything for four little girls. I
came to understand that even when we are powerless to save
ourselves, there are eyes that see and hands that move in
saving actions, carrying exponential returns.

Dad had given us his credit card and told us to go out to
lunch. "Do you think he'll mind that we picked such an
expensive place?" one of the sisters asks.

"He wouldn't want it any other way," I say.

Four girls raise their glasses, and they touch in the center.
The hands that hold them have come from far places.

"To Dad," one says.

"To Dad," say all the sisters.

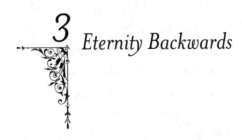

3 *Eternity Backwards*

My grandmother died at 7:00 A.M. Well, that was the time the people at the nursing home told us she died. It was also the time the shift changed. I have often wondered if that wasn't simply when someone found her dead.

I don't know if the dead can see us. But when I have thoughts about my grandmother, I have wished that they could. I would like to tell her how sorry I am that it ended so badly for her. When I have these thoughts, I hear her say, *I don't blame you, dear.*

In the Christian life there is little to be gained by focusing on regrets. But that is not to say there is no place in the Christian life for looking back. I have come to understand that eternity goes as far backward as it goes forward and that sometimes, in our forward-leaning orientation, we forget to look back and claim what others before us have bequeathed to us. Surely God intends such bequeathals, for he defined himself as the God of Abraham, Isaac, and Jacob—the God of the forebears, the ones who have "gone before."

My grandmother was demented when she died. And in the years preceding her death in 1986, she was in serious decline. So, as I have come to see it, I could not have realized the bequeathal then. It was after her death, when I was reading the volumes of journals she kept, that I discovered someone I hadn't known. That's when I took hold of my bequeathal. "We carry the voices of our ancestors in a way I don't understand," novelist and poet Diane Glancy told me once. "We are the voices of our grandmothers." When I came to recognize the voice of my grandmother in me, I found a piece of myself, too.

❋ ❋ ❋

My grandmother was born Pearl Bucklen in 1901, the oldest of six children in a family abandoned by their father when she was fourteen. She grew up in the hills of Freedom, Pennsylvania, near Pittsburgh, and married a railroad man and carpenter, Charles Bentel, in March 1925. Their first child, Lauralee, died in my grandmother's arms as a one-week-old infant, and they buried her in a cemetery high on a hill in Freedom and planted an evergreen sapling by her grave. My mother, Barbara, was born a few years later, and five years after that, her sister, my Aunt Sue, was born.

For a long time my sisters and I were Pearl Bucklen Bentel's only grandchildren. We knew her as Mema. "Pearl Bucklen Bentel" was a name on the vertical bindings of four novels. We knew she wrote books, but we knew other things better. Like the chocolate pudding she made (cooked, not instant) and put in delicate crystal bowls when we visited. Like the squat thrusts and leg lifts she did while watching Jack LaLane on television. The Scrabble games we played. The smell of raisin toast coming from her kitchen when she cooked our breakfast. The bowl of peanuts on the table in the living room (we ate them by the fistful). The *Woof! Woof! Woof!* she bellowed with ballooning cheeks from the backseat of a Land Rover making a sharp descent down a sand dune.

During the few years we knew her when she was still completely herself, one episode stands out in my mind as the point of entry into my "journey backwards." I was twelve, and my sister Carol and I had gone to Pennsylvania to spend Easter week with Mema and Pepa. Mema was writing a fifth novel during that time, and she asked me to read parts of it and offer my critique, which I did unabashedly. On the last page of chapter 3 I had casually commented that a certain dependent clause weakened the ending. "It would sound better without it," I told her.

I was sitting in a chair in her living room when she walked up to me, the pages of the manuscript, an inch thick, curled over her arm. She towered over me in her commanding way—tall, robust, bosomy, gangly, and a little goofy—and smiled. She pulled the pencil from her ear, found the page on which I had written my comment, and scribbled out the dependent clause—just like that. Then she stooped and kissed me on the cheek and thanked me for helping her make the book better.

I didn't know it then, but that became the defining moment through which I would find my bequeathal.

❀ ❀ ❀

Mema's journals begin in January 1940 and end in December 1979. These faded, worn, musty volumes contain four decades of self-disclosure and historical color. In broad strokes, her journals told me that the 1940s were her "radio" years, when she wrote scripts for radio soap operas and met and mentored Rod Serling, creator of *The Twilight Zone* and *Night Gallery*. The 1950s was the decade of her novels—and four granddaughters whose presence would challenge her writing life. She struggled in the 1960s with family illnesses and deaths. She also began to forget things. The 1970s saw a steady decline in her mental capacity. By the 1980s, for which there are no journals, she had lost herself. She no longer knew our names.

But it was the details of Mema's journals that offered glimpses into her soul and revealed the most to me about my grandmother the struggling writer. I learned, for example, that she wrestled with insecurities resulting from her father's abandonment; that she never went to college; that she had crooked teeth. She knew that she had been created to write, but so many other things got in the way. She found inspiration at the age of thirty-eight when she read *Peculiar Treasure* by Edna Ferber. It gave her "new incentive to go ahead, fight my way, no matter how slow." She already knew that she had to write. Now she knew that she had to *fight* to write.

During her early writing experiments, hammering out scripts for radio soap operas, she wrote a show she called "Howdy Stone" and sent a script to an agent—"W. S."—who was "bowled over" by it.

She wrote: "So!!! Thrills & sinking despair at the next episode to come on the air. Is this the turning point actually?"

As it turned out, "thrills and sinking despair" would define her writing life. She was a woman of the 1940s, after all, and had other commitments. She gave herself to the care and ministrations of her immediate and extended families, especially her mother, bearing an extra burden as the oldest child in the family abandoned by a father.

Pennsylvania winters didn't make it any easier. If Pearl wasn't sick in bed or tending to someone who was, she was shoveling snow. A journal entry on one winter's day noted, "Eighteen inches of the most beautiful drifted, confining snow I've ever seen. Beauty. Extravagance. Delight. Threw crumbs to the birds. Shoveled hours in the afternoon." The next day she wrote: "Spent most of Sunday in bed—not ill, completely exhausted. Chest hurting, such weariness." At the same time, "W. S." wasn't easy on her, constantly returning scripts and demanding rewrites.

A crushing setback occurred in 1942. Columbia Pictures had expressed an interest in one of her scripts, and trembling with anticipation, she bought a new blue hat to wear with her blue suit and traveled alone to New York. She felt "noticeably small-townish" but held her head high and pressed on. She met with the producer and then waited weeks before finally hearing a word. She received the script in the mail, unread, with a scribbled note saying he had never met the writer. "Have I been the victim of a hoax? I have found a new low in my 'career,'" she wrote.

There were some high points. By the mid-1940s she was writing two radio scripts a week for WCAE's half-hour radio program *Happiness Ahead*. Soon thereafter she took my mother to Antioch College in Yellow Springs, Ohio. There, Mema's life intersected with a young aspiring writer named Rod Serling, a classmate of my mother's. This would prove to be a highlight that would carry her even into her elderly years.

When Pearl Bentel visited the campus of Antioch in 1947 to visit her daughter Barb, Rod Serling sought her out. She noted in her journal: "He asked me to look at [scripts he had written], and I showed him enough to give him a vague idea of what I was writing. I said if he'd think of something that would fit in, I'd pay him for an episode. What he wrote showed me he knew how to write and could write his own show one day. I used five or six of his scripts (after deleting, changing, etc.) and paid him." She grew accustomed to "her eager student waiting for her with a batch of fresh scripts" during subsequent Antioch visits, notes Serling biographer Gordon Sander in his book *Serling, the Rise and Twilight of Television's Last Angry Man*.

By the end of the decade Mema's focus had shifted from radio to juvenile fiction. She started her first novel in 1948, spurred on by friends and neighbors. Her good friends the Weirs had a bell on their kitchen stoop and told her to come over and ring the bell when she finished her first book. That way everyone in the neighborhood would know and could celebrate with her. On June 17, 1948, her journal reads, "Went out into the bright sunshine and rang the Weirs' bell."

❈ ❈ ❈

Her first novel, *Program for Christine*, sold in January 1952. (She rang the Weirs' bell then, too.) The following March the novel became that year's Junior Literary Guild selection, something I had to read her journals to find out. By this time she had a new agent, Betty, and had to make frequent train trips to Chicago with manuscripts to meet with her. Before leaving on these trips, she fretted about baking "cookies for Chuck" and "kuchen to take to Sue" and was always late getting out the door. After the baking and fretting for one particular trip, she finished typing the short story "Mother Had Other Ideas" late into the night, which almost made her miss her train. I would like to have read that story.

Granddaughter number one—"Susie"—was born in October of 1953.

My grandmother's first royalty check (for $310.45) arrived two years later, just as she was completing her second novel, *I'll Know My Love.* Happy as she was at its selling, she was shocked and distraught to see the cover the publisher had picked for that novel. "Such an ugly girl. . . . She isn't my idea of the girl I wrote about, at all."

Along came granddaughter number two—Wendy—in January 1956, with "much black hair, squirming, sucking mouth." A little more than a year later in May, granddaughter number three was born, my sister Carol: "A lusty beautiful black-haired blue-eyed triplicate of the other two."

She finished her third novel, *Co-Ed Off Campus,* in December of that same year: "Stayed at typewriter—all week, from Mon. to Sat. Worked madly to correct incomplete angles. Tore sheet out of typewriter 8:00 P.M. Read—corrected—assembled & sealed it at 1:40 *Sat morning.*" It is easy to forget that back then, writing involved a lot of backspacing and carbon paper.

When she received word from a publisher that they liked the third novel but it was "diffuse" and had to be cut by fifty pages, she was "madder, even, than crushed, yet crushed—crushed" that they wanted her to cut a section about "religion."

She settled down a few days later—"quieter—saner—will shorten it, of course"—but held her ground on the religion part, refusing to delete it. This novel sold in 1959, the same year that grand-daughter number four, Nancy, was born. She was different from the other three: "long, wiry, perfect, with Chuck's reddish hair—not long & dark as with the others." And she noted in her journals that at last she had found her writing voice: "*At last—at last—now I know* what I must do! More teen-age novels—more, more, *more.*"

But "more, more, more" was not to be. By the 1960s, with the four granddaughters populating her life, her writing slowed, and her life became filled with other distractions and heartaches. Her journals took a noticeable dark turn in this decade, as in the poem she wrote titled "November":

> *Scowl on, angry skies,*
> *And knit your brow in sullen ugliness!*
> *'Twill match my mood!*
> *Keep pelting, chill relentless rain*
> *Until you have dispelled*
> *This fog of densest muddleness*
> *that has so long confused my brain.*
> *Stark ugliness of fall,*
> *Strip now last vestige of deceptive bloom*
> *From this my heart*
> *In springtime wooed.*

Her own seriously low blood pressure and the threat of a stroke, along with a string of family illnesses and deaths and four granddaughters hounding her slowed and frustrated her writing life, reducing it to fits and starts. Now her journals were filled with notations like, "Simply can't understand how the time has flown without my accomplishing a thing" and "Why am I not doing what I want above all else?" She dropped her book club and women's club, but family obligations consumed any gains she made.

She reached a critical juncture in 1963 when her former protégé, Rod Serling, was teaching a writing seminar at Antioch College. Evidently because of health concerns, my grandfather did not want her to attend it, and they exchanged words about it. "He still thinks it's too much for my energy." She battled similar concerns herself: "I wonder, too, will it be too much?"

She was sixty-two years old. She knew it wouldn't be easy to make the trip to Yellow Springs, Ohio, by herself in the dead of winter and live with college students for several weeks. At the same time, for so many years she had allowed other urgencies to eat away the focus and resolve needed to realize her own call. She worried about having the energy to make the trip and meet the demands of the seminar. At the same time, she asked herself, "Should I go on using *more* energy—piddling away on phone calls—social gestures—cleaning the house—shopping? I simply can't submit to strangling every impulse to doing what is *my life—my* interest. What do I have to give Circle—church—neighbors—even family—that I haven't already given?"

She went to the seminar, traveling alone by train, in January 1963. It proved to be a high point—and the only portion of her journals where she ran out of space on the pages. Her entries are replete with enthusiastic notations:

January 9: "Surprise moment when Rod Serling announced that the first person who paid real money for a script of his— Pearl Bentel—was right over there (& he pointed to me)! 'She bought the very first script I ever sold.'"

January 11: [At an evening party after a class]: "As a result of Rod's surprising announcement, I had constant companionship at the party—these eager young men each with *his* idea of what he wanted to write. And each is so talented—so eager to hear what experience has to teach—& so intent on *using* their talent. (All so much better educated than I—I felt quite humble.)"

January 30: "Last meeting of the seminar. Rod threw the meeting open to questions, & much concrete information was forthcoming. He said *if* we ever wrote anything we *knew* was good & if it was the best writing we could do—to send it to his first agent . . . and to his present one, saying 'old Rod told us to.' He also gave the class his home address, saying if the above was true, *he* would read it."

She wrote a paragraph within the same pages, in quotation marks with no attribution, that seems to have been some parting words from their illustrious instructor, Rod Serling:

Being a writer is a frustrating business—eats U up—a desperately lonely occupation—there is no one there but you. . . .There comes not once, but many times,

that terrifying moment when you can't write. You think—
Have I come to the end? Have I run dry? Now I'll never
be a writer again. . . . There are rewards—that of knowing what you've just finished is the best you can do.

It was, she noted, a "most satisfying & stimulating seminar."
She hated the cover of her third novel, published in 1959.
In any case, it got good reviews, for which she was grateful.
Her fourth novel sold in 1964; she called it *Co-Ed Off Campus.*
Soon, however, the memory problems started. "My eyes keep
twitching; I can't type as long as I used to anymore! Oh,
age—and if it's not bad enough to be always forgetting." In
April 1968 she jotted highlights of the week my sister and I
spent at her and Pepa's house over Easter, the week she gave
me the manuscript to read and I gave her my "advice."
"Wendy & Carol unpacked—helped with dinner & dishes—
and we played Hands Down and another card game."

That week would be the last time I saw my grandfather.
On June 10, 1968, Mema opened her journal entry:
"Chuck awakened ill—" That date, for her, was the begin-
ning of the end:

As we were dressing to go to Dr. Johnson about 4 P.M.,
I spoke from front room to him as he was dressing in
back room—as we had been doing, back & forth. He
didn't answer and I rushed into the back bedroom. He
was lying back on the edge of the bed, dressed in trou-
sers, undershirt & socks—his shoes on the floor as if he
intended putting them on—one foot on the floor as if

he had just leaned back. I called his name—I clasped his head—his lips were warm—I ran to Betty Lindsey's screaming for her to call the doctor. He came at once—said, "he's gone."—my Chuck—

Her life seemed to me like a blur after that. We moved her out of her house that summer to be closer to us in Ohio, and we took her on a month-long camping trip out west. That was when she went down the sand dune in the Land Rover. After that her *Woof! Woof! Woof!* became a standard mode of expression for my sister and me for years to come.

We knew she missed Pepa because sometimes she'd cry. But she hid it more than she showed it. She wrote shortly after he died: "Slept alone in our double room with *no* weird feelings. It is good, good, to know that he did not rouse & have to live with incapacities. I'm all right. He is everywhere and I recall so many directions he gave me as to how to do this & that. Still can't figure out the timer for the lamp in the front window. *Why* am I so confused? Is it apparent to everyone?"

Her journals of the 1970s are filled with reflections of Pepa. June 10, 1970: "Just two years ago this afternoon—Chuck died. And now I'm alone—still trying to collect thoughts, working hard on my manuscript. Perhaps my ability to think and create with words has really been shattered ever since."

She titled her unpublished fifth novel *You Can Do* (with a personal subscript: "without a degree, without a father, without a beautician, [with] crooked teeth"). That novel came back with a rejection slip: "A blow but no tears. It was what I expected—not relevant any longer."

She attended an address by Rod Serling at the University of Akron that same year. (He acknowledged her from the podium.) She also failed her driver's test that year ("too nervous—and too wide a curve in making turns. Quite a blow"). We took her to see *Godspell* in 1972 ("Jesus quotations against noisy background"), and by the end of that year she was making notes about where she was putting things: Her Eisenhower dollars were in the "4th drawer r. chest." The china Easter egg, "top shelf rear above dishwasher." Reserve vitamins, "Bottom shelf in hall." Her Christmas list that year included Jergens hand lotion and a whisk broom. She wrote near the end of the year: "So confused—so tired—I do miss Chuck more than ever & am glad he doesn't see me—so forgetful—"

Rod Serling died in 1975. My grandmother kept a framed black-and-white photo of him on her wall until she moved into the nursing home.

A man named Frank appeared in later entries. Apparently his family didn't approve of the courtship and pressured him to move into a nursing home, which he resisted. Frank wanted to marry my grandmother. But although she enjoyed their talks and visits, she turned him down. Their relationship lasted for five years. He disappeared one day without another word to her, and her final mention of him appears in the entry dated August 28, 1979: "Haven't heard from him. Think he's in a nursing home."

She wrote her last poem at my request, for our first son, Nathanael, born October 1979:

Beloved child, the hours we've
waited for your coming
have been filled with love
and gratitude,
With neither doubt nor fear—
But only joy and thankfulness
And now, at last—you're here!
Our prayers have all been answered.
So welcome, tiny little one
Come home with us
and share our joy.

Her last journal entry was dated December 26, 1979: "Christmas at Barb's—lovely—"

❊ ❊ ❊

I encountered some surprises reading my grandmother's journals, the most notable being the romance and intimacy she shared with my grandfather. The first clue came in the list of the items she bought before her marriage, things like "a paring knife" and "a knife sharpener," "a sugar spoon" and the "teddies": "A crepe nightie. A vail teddy. A white teddy. A flesh teddy."

Seeing so much heartache in her own family, she wrote of her marriage that "only we are lucky and happy." Among her papers and journals I found a brown-edged tattered envelope with the word *Sweetheart* written on it. It contained this letter, penned by my grandfather on February 14, 1928:

Sweetie Pie:

This is Valentine's Day and wouldn't be complete without asking you to be mine. Honey, it's nearly three years since we became each others "'Til death do us part" and, dear, there has been no time in my life that I wanted you more than right now. Sweetheart, I love you more and more and more and now that you're doing for me and us what you wouldn't do for anyone else, I love you still more. Darling, you don't think me foolish but I have been thinking, thinking how happy we're going to be with our baby when it comes. Remember, dear, how happy we were with sweet Lauralee before she went away from us? Honey, I'm crying but only because I'm happy I have you and because Lauralee doesn't have to go through this wicked old world and fight to live. Darling, I'm happy because you love me. (You do, don't you?)

Lovingly always yours,

"Chuck"

I never knew that side of my grandfather. I never knew they had been so in love. How could I have known? Still, I wish I had.

The last time I saw my grandmother was on January 27, 1986, my thirtieth birthday. She was in a hospital with tubes everywhere, laboring for every breath, breathing sporadically. I didn't think she'd live through the night, but she lived four more months. It must have been Jack LaLane and all those vitamins.

By the time she died, she hardly knew any of us. She retreated further and further into the recesses of her failing mind. Sometimes she'd cry and mumble about being a burden, and she'd talk about going back to Pennsylvania. She never did go back once she had reached that condition, not until we took her back to bury her next to the man who had preceded her in death by eighteen years. The evergreen tree they planted for Lauralee towered over all the others.

She once wrote a poem called "Pennsylvania":

Ah, Pennsylvania, bountiful
Extend your blithesome thrill
To every restless traveler, threading
in and out
Your highways, dipping, climbing
Round each wooded hill
And mountain, that he might have his fill
Of beauty you so freely spread about,
Share the quiet of your valleys,
The hushed murmurs of your woods.

She didn't know much else those last years of her life, but she knew she wanted to go back there. I used to go to the nursing home and read the Scriptures to her, and sometimes I felt sure that was bringing her back. She would begin to remember me, and I thought if we all worked hard at bringing out what was left, maybe she would come back to us. Maybe that squat-thrusting, Scrabble-loving, *Woof-woof-woofing,* goofy grandmother who made us get our prepositions right and who stored a treasury of vitamin Cs would come to life again. That impetuous woman who took train trips to New York and Chicago and Ohio and who bought hats and wore suits and mentored Rod Serling and refused to delete religion out of one of the five novels she authored. That towering woman who asked me, a twelve-year-old, for advice on chapter 3.

I do believe the dead see us. It says so in the New Testament book of Hebrews. They are the "cloud of witnesses." They are the ones who went before, who did not receive what was promised. They looked for it. They longed for it. They moved in the direction of it. But they did not take hold of it. That would be left to the ones who follow.

In the final chapter of *The Brothers Karamazov* the lead character, Alyosha, is speaking to children who are attending the funeral of a friend, another child. They are weeping and missing their friend, and Alyosha says, "I want you to understand, then, that there is nothing nobler, stronger, healthier, and more helpful in life than a good remembrance, particularly a remembrance from our childhood. . . . I feel that a beautiful, holy memory preserved from early childhood can be the most important single thing in our development. . . . Even if we have only one such memory, it is possible that it will be enough to save us some day."

She slipped a pencil from her ear. She crossed out the dependent clause. She kissed my cheek and thanked me. Part of her was draining away, and the same part was awakening inside me. I wish I had loved her more. I could have brought her back to Pennsylvania, and she could have looked over those rolling hills and felt the presence and power of home. I wish I could have told her how sorry I am that it ended so badly for her.

I don't blame you, dear. Take the pencil from my ear. Fight your way, no matter how slow.

4 *Kelly's Gift*

In the summer of 1972 I took a Greyhound bus cross-country from Ohio to Dallas, Texas. I had joined a group of fellow "Jesus Freaks" bound for Explo '72, a weeklong evangelism training program sponsored by Campus Crusade for Christ. "Give me oil for my lamp; keep me burnin', burnin', burnin'" was the mantra of the week, one of the many funky praise choruses that helped define the Jesus movement back then. We greeted one another not with the standard hippie "peace sign" but with the innovative single raised index finger, "one way," the Jesus sign.

At Explo we attended workshops and praisefests. I learned how to "witness," something I hadn't done before: You take a little yellow booklet called *The Four Spiritual Laws*; you knock on people's doors or turn to them on an airplane or in a movie theater, and say, "Have you heard of *The Four Spiritual Laws?*" They'll say no. (Prior to Explo '72 hardly anyone, anywhere, had heard of *The Four Spiritual Laws*.) After they say no, you pull out the little yellow booklet and read the laws to them. It doesn't take long. We learned at the workshops how to expedite the process. Then, after they've heard the laws, you ask them if they have a relationship with Jesus Christ. If they haven't already stopped you by this point, they'll say no. Then you say, "Would you like to pray the prayer here in the booklet and receive him?"

I returned from Explo empowered and armed with a suitcase full of little yellow booklets and promptly undertook practice sessions with easy targets before I launched into the world of meeting strangers in movie theaters.

I hoodwinked my sister Carol, then fifteen, into coming with me to the swing set in our backyard. We bobbed and dangled with a summer breeze in our faces as I pulled out my little yellow booklet.

She hadn't heard of *The Four Spiritual Laws:*

1. God loves you and has a wonderful plan for your life.
2. Man is sinful and separated from God, and cannot know God or experience his love and wonderful plan.
3. Jesus Christ is God's only provision to bridge this separation.
4. We must individually receive Jesus Christ as Savior and Lord to derive the benefits of God's love and plan.

"Would you like to pray the prayer here in the booklet and receive him?"

Without a moment's hesitation she said she wanted to pray the prayer. So I read it. She repeated it. I prayed. She prayed. She cried. I cried.

The Lord had been effectually "received." We then proceeded to the matter of the Fact-Faith-Feeling train highlighted at the back of the booklet. The *fact* of what God has done through Christ is the engine that drives the train, I said. *Fact* pulls *faith*, which would be like, say, the dining car. *Feelings*, the booklet said, take up the rear; they are the caboose. "The caboose must never drive the train," I told my sister.

❋ ❋ ❋

Of the four sisters Carol and I were closest in age, being a little more than a year apart. This naturally caused our worlds to intersect at nearly every point. I can't think of a childhood memory without her. The summer days of our childhood were filled with expeditions to the vacant lots behind our neighbor's house—we called it "the field"—where we built forts and learned curse words. We explored "the big log" in the nearby woods, and on our front patio we built spaceships out of plywood, sometimes sleeping there during weekends (with "space walks" on Saturday nights to watch *Mission Impossible*).

Our lives were no less entwined during our high school years. If she hadn't allowed Andy Parker to mimeograph and distribute her Latin translations for everyone in Latin 1 my sophomore year, I never would have made it to Latin 2. We harmonized on Monkees songs and put together a version of *Godspell*'s "All for the Best" that, we had no doubt, could have won us a spot on *The Gene Carroll Show*, a local amateur talent program. We performed a lively version of Ike and Tina

Turner's "Proud Mary." Carol was Ike—she could reach the low note on the "rollin'" echo; I was Tina—I could shimmy.

Our closeness took a strange turn in our adult years. We had differing goals, and our lives went in opposite directions. Carol attended college and graduate school in the South, where she eventually married and settled. I stayed north.

Her choices felt foreign to me after a lifetime of sharing everything. I convinced myself that this was how it was supposed to be. People grow up. They go their own way. That was life, but it was disorienting. I didn't like it. I missed my sister. I didn't know how to navigate the passages of my life without her. Anyway, that's the way we lived for several years— she in the South, surrounded by good friends with lazy drawls, sipping sweet tea and wearing Laura Ashley dresses; I in New Jersey, battling through "Armpit of the Nation" jokes and trying to make ends meet on a pastor's salary, with three young sons who tended to break furniture. Sometimes we'd touch base by phone, but I couldn't afford hefty phone bills, so weeks—sometimes months—could pass without our talking. Our lives were pulling us into different spheres.

❋ ❋ ❋

Then, on the fourth of July 1987 just as my husband, Bob, and our young sons and I returned home from a picnic, the phone rang. It was my youngest sister, Nancy. "Kelly fell. She's in the hospital. It doesn't look like it's life-threatening."

I wondered why she would bring the words "life-threatening" into it. Firecrackers popped in the background.

Kelly was Carol's little girl, her firstborn child. She was

just three days away from her second birthday, on July 7. The boys and I had started to make her birthday cards.

"Carol, Tim, and Kelly were away for the weekend at a condo," Nancy continued. "Kelly got out of bed this morning and wandered over to look out the window. She put her hands on the screen. It wasn't secured, and she fell about ten feet. She landed on her head on the concrete."

Kelly was transferred by helicopter to the pediatric intensive care unit at a hospital in Asheville, North Carolina, where Carol and Tim lived. Nancy gave me the phone number, and I called right away. Carol was shaken but composed.

"We need to pray that the swelling on her brain will go down," she said.

"Do you want me to come?"

"I don't know," she said. "Just pray."

We didn't talk long. I gathered the boys and Bob, and we got on our knees around our bed. "Dear Lord, help cousin Kelly feel better," Ben prayed. "Dear Lord, help her brain not swell," said Nathanael. We all prayed, and when we were finished, Bob looked at me and said, "You should go."

The rest of the night was a blur. I got a flight out of Newark to Asheville, via Charlotte, for the following morning. I couldn't focus on what to pack. I expected to be gone only a few days, to take care of Carol's new baby boy, James, and cover the home front while Kelly recovered in the hospital. I stopped momentarily in front of my closet, looking at my church clothes. I decided I wouldn't need any.

We roused our children at 4:00 in the morning and piled them into the car so Bob could get me to the airport in time to make my 6:00 A.M. flight. "Make some pretty cards for cousin Kelly, and send them to her for her birthday. She'll like that," I told the boys.

I made my connection in Charlotte and nearly vomited on the bumpy commuter plane. If I hadn't been able to beg saltines off a bartender upon my arrival, I'm sure I would have heaved. Tim's mother met me and drove me to the hospital. She explained that after Kelly fell, she had remained conscious for several minutes. She sang "Itsy-Bitsy Spider" and knew her baby brother James's name. Then she lost consciousness. As we neared the hospital, Tim's mother told me, "I've already said my good-byes."

The next thing I knew, I was being led through heavy doors onto the pediatric floor. The waiting area was filled with teary-eyed people I didn't know. They asked me, "Are you Carol's sister?" We walked through more doors, past more people with red noses and puffy eyes. I was taken into a room with a sign on the door that said No Admittance. There was my sister Carol with her husband, Tim. And Kelly. She was lying on the bed, unconscious.

Carol cried in my arms. "I don't think she's going to make it."

I wasn't prepared to hear that.

I went to Kelly. For a long time I looked at her. It had been over a year since I had seen her. I took her little hand, and I stroked her arm and her hair. Her face was swollen and bruised. There were tubes everywhere, tubes in her arms, her mouth, her nose, and a respirator kept time like a metronome as it pumped life into her lungs.

"You're a good girl, Kelly. We all love you."

My parents, my brother, Chris, and sister Sue arrived later that day; Nancy, later that night. We stood in the hallway, hugging and crying. We took turns going in and staying with Kelly. After a while we didn't see the tubes or the bruises, and we didn't hear the rhythm of the respirator. We settled into the PICU as if it were a second home.

Now and then Kelly's monitors would beep. At first this alarmed us. It meant something wasn't working right. We looked on frantically as the nurses casually adjusted this tube or that button. In time we grew accustomed to hearing those beeps.

People from my sister's church came and prayed over Kelly. The pastor and elders invited us to join them around her bed to lay hands on her and pray. My father and I were expecting a miracle.

Later Tim's father, Bill, was reading aloud from Psalm 27: "One thing I ask of the Lord, this is what I seek: that I may dwell in the house of the Lord all the days of my life, to gaze upon the beauty of the Lord and to seek him in his temple."

Then Kelly moved her leg.

"Did you see that?" I said to my father, standing next to me.

"Keep reading, Bill," my father said. "I think she may hear it."

Carol and Tim, who had been resting in the waiting area, appeared immediately when they got word that Kelly had moved.

Bill kept reading: "He will keep me safe in his dwelling; he will hide me in the shelter of his tabernacle and set me high upon a rock."

We called the nurse.

"She moved her leg. It wasn't a twitch. She bent it all the way up and then straightened it," I said.

I rubbed Kelly's arms and told her she was a good girl. "Try to move your leg again, honey. Come back to us, Kelly. We're here for you."

"KELLY, CAN YOU MOVE YOUR LEG?" the nurse said in a loud voice. She was tapping Kelly's leg. "KELLY, HONEY, MOVE THIS LEG."

Kelly didn't respond.

I looked at the nurse plaintively. "Maybe she's trying, but she can't tell us she's trying."

"She may be trying real hard," the nurse said.

Kelly didn't move her leg again.

Slowly, in painful, measured moments of relinquishment, it became clear we weren't going to get a miracle. Talk of miracles only made it harder for Carol and Tim. Carol started talking about funeral arrangements. I couldn't fathom how a mother could say the word *funeral* in the same sentence with the name of her child. They had tried desperately to keep Kelly conscious in the ambulance. That's when she sang "Itsy-Bitsy Spider." But it was only a matter of minutes before she lost consciousness. Carol seemed to understand better than the rest of us that Kelly was not going to come back to us.

A friend of Tim's family had hosted all the Murrays in their big house near the hospital. During those first days we hardly slept. We came and went in shifts to and from the hospital, meeting one another in darkened hallways of that house, looking for car keys and jackets, roused without the help of alarm clocks. During the few hours I was able to fade in and out of twilight sleep, I dreamt Kelly opened her eyes and looked at me. It woke me.

What would it take for God to grant us this miracle? Some kind of confession to clean the slate? *I renounce all my petty complaints. I promise I won't harbor anymore critical thoughts. Please bring Kelly back. Please let Kelly open her eyes.* Somehow, in those desperate moments I knew my petty complaints and critical thoughts had nothing to do with what we were facing.

I awoke before dawn on July 6. I heard myself say, *Kelly is going to die today.* The doctors held a family meeting in an empty hospital room. All the Murrays and most of Tim's family, the Harrisons, were there. The doctors were kind, measured, and forthright. They explained why there was no hope for Kelly's recovery. The swelling in her head had cut off the circulation to her brain, they said. The EEG showed no brain activity. The leg movement was a spastic response of the nervous system. We sat and listened, numb, exhausted, stricken, and light-headed. We nodded. Kelly is going to die today. The doctors were helping us figure that out. Today was the day we would say our good-byes. The family meeting brought us to the edge of what we knew we had to do. The respirator was keeping her alive, really, to give the family time to assimilate the tragedy and to say our good-byes to a warm, sleeping child.

That day, the day before Kelly's second birthday, we said good-bye.

By the time my husband, Bob, arrived, Kelly was gone.

Carol and Tim asked him to help with the graveside commit-
tal service, which would be for family only. The pastor of
Tim and Carol's church would handle the public memorial
service to be held later the same day.

The next day, Kelly's second birthday, Carol and Tim did
not lay out the party favors and birthday hats Carol had
already purchased. Instead, they called the florist, picked the
cemetery plot, and planned the memorial service.

My mother took the sisters shopping. None of us had
brought church clothes, so shopping seemed like the thing to
do. Carol couldn't make any decisions about what dress to
buy. She didn't want to wear black (to defy death's victory),
but we found a simple black-and-white print dress with a
white collar. It worked. Carol wore red shoes and a red pin
on the white collar as her statement of defiance.

Kelly was buried the next day in the Easter dress Carol had
made her. She looked surprisingly good as she lay in her
pint-sized casket. The swelling was gone. Her cheeks were
ruddy and fat. Her skin was soft. This comforted us. Carol
stood next to her and laid her "blankey" across her chest.
"Here darlin', here's your blankey," she said. She tucked it
under Kelly's arm and fussed over the ruffles on her Easter
dress.

We buried her on a typical July day in North Carolina.
The casket seemed too small to be perched over that big
hole, so precariously high on such massive supports.

Bob opened in prayer. His voice was strained. I could tell
he was trying not to cry. "The prophet Jeremiah says in his
Lamentations:

He has broken my teeth with gravel; he has trampled me
in the dust. I have been deprived of peace; I have
forgotten what prosperity is. So I say, "My splendor is
gone and all that I had hoped from the Lord." I
remember my affliction and my wandering, the bitterness and the gall. I well remember them, and my soul is
downcast within me. Yet this I call to mind and therefore I have hope: Because of the Lord's great love we are
not consumed, for his compassions never fail. They are
new every morning; great is your faithfulness. I say to
myself, "The Lord is my portion; therefore I will wait
for him."

Bob continued, "Jesus said, 'Let the little children come
to me, and do not hinder them.' For reasons we cannot
understand, God sent us a visiting angel for one year and
364 days. Why so short a time? Why only two years? We want
to ask these kinds of questions."

Kelly understands the answers now, I remember thinking. *And we
are left behind without answers.*

"We have only this to hang on to," Bob was saying. "His
compassions are new every morning. All the mornings for
the rest of our lives we will ask God for enough of his
compassion to get us through another day.

"Carol has told me that Kelly used to sing Jesus songs," he
said toward his conclusion. "One of her favorites was 'Jesus
Loves Me.' When the great German theologian Karl Barth
was once asked how he would summarize what it means to be
a believer in Christ, he answered with the words to this

simple song. Let's sing it together now, in remembrance of Kelly's own confession of faith in God when she sang it. Let us stand on the hope that even in a moment like this, that confession is true."

There were probably twenty of us standing there facing the small white casket. Some of us knew all about church. Others made no pretense about being religious. We stood, old and young, religious and nonreligious, and sang Kelly's confession. Cicadas served as background music, and the breeze blew our dresses. Sometimes we struggled to reach the right note. Sometimes the notes got swallowed in our throats.

> *Jesus loves me! this I know,*
> *For the Bible tells me so;*
> *Little ones to him belong;*
> *They are weak, but he is strong.*

Bob returned to New Jersey the next day. The rest of the family stayed with Carol through the weekend. My mother, sisters, and I purchased new bedroom furniture for Kelly's room and rearranged it so it looked different. We helped Carol go through Kelly's things. Carol didn't want to throw away Kelly's pink toothbrush. I packed it in a Ziploc bag. Nancy and I were going through the coat closet when we pulled out Kelly's mittens tucked way in the back. We looked at one another. Neighbors dropped by with cards and nut breads, and the mailman was heartsick when he learned the little girl who lived at this address had died. He was delivering her birthday cards.

By the end of the first week our parents had returned home, and Sue left soon after. Then Nancy followed. I felt my sister's supports coming out from under her with each departure. I stayed on for another week.

The days got harder. The remembrance of a life lost pervaded this home. I missed my sons. Carol and I went to Kelly's grave. It was smaller than the other fresh graves nearby. The flowers from the memorial service were still there, but they had withered, including the four pink roses my boys and her other cousin had given to rest on top of her casket.

Carol insisted on returning the party favors. She held the receipt in her trembling hand and slid it onto the counter. The store clerk was skeptical. I was prepared to intervene. *Look, these favors were for her little girl's birthday party, and she died. Just give her back her money.*

It didn't come to that. We got through it. Carol had long ago abandoned any embarrassment about crying in public.

We looked through photographs of Kelly to put in a book. Carol lingered over them and touched Kelly's face. I couldn't bear watching her look at Kelly's pictures, wishing she could hold her again, knowing all she had were glossy images on cardboard. She told me she longed for heaven so she could see her little girl again. "I know I shouldn't think that. I should want to be there to praise God," she said. I told her that God would be praised seeing a mother and her daughter reunited and singing his praises together.

I longed for the normalcy of my own family but could barely face the thought of the day when I had to leave my

sister. *How will she get up in the mornings? How will she get through a day?*
A friend of Carol's and I arranged for church people to
drop by every day on a systematic basis for as long as needed.
They promised me they would. I promised Carol I would
come back with the boys later in the summer.

She stood with Tim in the airport and waved as I walked
through the gate. The best I could do was toss a glance and
wave back. I tried to swallow, but I felt as if a grapefruit had
settled in my throat. I pushed back the tears while I sat at the
gate, waiting to board.

The commuter flight from Asheville to Charlotte was
much smoother. I looked out the window at the red earth
and scanned the mountainsides, wondering where Kelly's
grave might be. I had said good-bye to her, once in the
hospital room, and a second time as she lay like a flower in
her little casket. This was the third time, looking out the
window at those indifferent mountains.

❄ ❄ ❄

I was home, but I was not ready to reenter the world I had
left the day I packed my suitcase without taking church
clothes. Part of me seemed to be someplace else. Unexpected
flashes of memory would overtake me. Strange moments
from our ordeal would come flooding back in my memory.
Once I was choosing bananas in the produce section of the
Food Lion when I found myself back in the hospital cafeteria
with my father, mother, and Sue. We were discussing
whether Carol and Tim ought to keep Kelly's play kitchen
set. I was standing in the kitchen ironing a blouse when I

found myself in the PICU, holding Kelly on my lap, rubbing her fat legs, and trying to keep her head up because her neck was limp. So many tears fell onto the blouse I was ironing that I had to put it away.

How does one carry the weight of grief? I did not grieve so much for my lost niece, though I loved her and missed her. The weight I bore was grief for my sister. She couldn't carry the weight of her grief alone. Somehow, strangely, I took it on. Carol's grief became mine.

Every week for a year after Kelly died, I called Carol, and I wrote her a letter. That way she would hear from me twice a week. It would give her a reason to stand on two legs, put one foot in front of the other, and walk to the mailbox. It would give her a reason to pick up the phone when it rang. I rallied the boys to send her and Tim pictures of Kelly in heaven and letters and poems, anything to keep them going to the mailbox and opening envelopes. Ben, who was five, wrote Kelly a letter: "Dear Kelly, What do you do in heaven? Do they have swimming pools? Do you walk on sidewalks? Is Moses up there? Is Daniel up there? Do you know these guys? Are there trees? How old are you in heaven? Are you two? Do you know everything in heaven? Can you see everything? Can you see me? Do you have your own room? Is there a man named Pop there? Do you know everybody's name?"

Those were the practical manifestations. The greater burden of grief was expressed in the groanings of my heart. There were days I fasted for my sister and her husband, days I wrote prayers for them in my journal. I thought, *If I write out the prayers, it will make them more real:* "Dear Lord, touch my sister with your power and strength. I don't know how to pray, other than to sigh and moan. These are groans too deep for words. Save her. How can this pain, this constant hurt, be transformed into a miracle, for my niece's mother?"

The following February Carol told me, "It's been eight months since I've seen my daughter, and the pain only gets worse. Is there ever a time when it won't hurt?" I told her I didn't know if it would ever not hurt for her again.

I talked to Tim on the phone one time when he was having "a bad day." He called to the Lord, who led him to read Psalm 31: "I will be glad and rejoice in your love, for you saw my affliction and knew the anguish of my soul. . . . Be merciful to me, O Lord, for I am in distress; my eyes grow weak with sorrow, my soul and my body with grief. . . . But I trust in you, O Lord; I say, 'You are my God.' My times are in your hands; . . . Let your face shine on your servant; save me in your unfailing love."

When my sister and I talked, she would ask things like, "What do you think she is doing now?" She would tell me about the acquaintances who didn't know how to respond and, so, didn't say anything at all. We talked about the mystery of life and death and tragedy in a world where lawns are mowed, the mail gets delivered, and library books are returned. "Some people say I'm privileged that God chose me for this," she said to me once. "I don't see it that way." We explored strange themes like "the fellowship of [Christ's] suffering" and the "blessedness" of those who mourn.

Mostly, though, we just hurt together.

❅ ❅ ❅

That same summer our youngest son, Jon, who was four,
found a baby squirrel in the driveway. Its eyes were shut, and
it was barely breathing. Jon put plastic bags on his hands,
picked up the squirrel, and put it in a shoe box, which we
kept on the front porch. Jon named him Walnut.

By late in the day Walnut had revived. He was crawling
around, and his eyes were open. Sometimes he squealed and
chirped. This sent Jon into fits. He begged us to let him
bring Walnut into the house. If Walnut squealed, Jon
instantly appeared at his side to comfort him. He chopped
peanuts for Walnut and gave him milk in a spoon.

We were amazed to see Walnut still breathing when we
checked him the next morning. He was even showing signs of
strength. "We saved a life, Jon," I said.

But Saturday afternoon Walnut had taken a turn for the
worse. Jon came running into the house screaming and
crying. "Flies are all over him," he said.

When Bob went to look, he concluded sadly that Walnut
was almost dead. I couldn't bear to see it. By the time I went
outside, an hour later, Jon had already buried Walnut. I
asked him to show me the grave. He took me to the spot in
the side yard, where he had buried Walnut under a tree. "I'm
gonna wait and then dig him up and put his bones in my
room," he said.

That evening Jon wept bitter tears. "I keep thinking about
Walnut. I miss him."

I sat him on my lap while we read the Bible as a family

after supper. Bob read the passage about the royal officer whose son lay sick to the point of death. The officer pleaded with Jesus to heal his son: "Sir, come down before my child dies." Jesus told him that his son would live.

"Why didn't God heal Walnut?" Jon asked Bob.

I wanted to ask the same thing about Kelly. Why didn't God heal Kelly? The prayers and pleas of my sister and her husband were no less earnest than those of the officer who pleaded for his son.

"He healed Walnut so that he would never need healing again," Bob said to Jon. "I'll bet when Walnut went to heaven, cousin Kelly picked him up and kept him with her since her cousin Jon took such good care of him," he said. "Cousin Kelly may be playing with Walnut right now in heaven."

Jon stopped crying and sat quietly for a few minutes. Then out of nowhere, he buried his face in my shoulder and cried again, "I still miss him. I can't see him anymore."

"It hurts to lose someone, honey." I was crying too.

"Why does it have to hurt so much?"

"When we love, we take a risk. But love is what makes us human. When we suffer because of love, it makes us more human," Bob said.

After our prayers Jon went to the dining room and took the framed picture of Kelly. She was sitting on the front step, clutching a daffodil, and glancing at the camera with an impish grin.

"When I miss Walnut, I'm going to look at cousin Kelly," he said.

He took the photo to his room and put it on his dresser. As I tucked him into his bed, he looked at me with swollen eyes. "Mom, does your mind control everything?"

"No. It controls a lot, but it doesn't control everything."

"The Holy Spirit is like the helper, right?" he said.

"Yes, he's the helper," I said. "The Holy Spirit will help your missing Walnut." I kissed and hugged him. He slept soundly the rest of the night.

Later that summer I took the boys back to visit my sister. They hadn't seen Carol and Tim since Kelly died. The next few days we picked wineberries on Mount Mitchell, devouring more than we salvaged for ice cream back home. We went swimming in the icy waters of Tim's old haunt, Baby Slidin' Rock. We caught trout by the ten pounds at a trout farm and cooked them on the grill.

The day before we left, I took the boys to the cemetery to visit Kelly's grave. Tim had chosen the spot, next to a freshly planted redbud sapling at the base of a knoll.

Kelly's name and her short life span were carved into the stone, as if establishing her loss forever. Carol and Tim also had engraved Jesus' words: "Let the children come to me, and do not hinder them."

The boys and I put flowers on the stone and sat down on the grass. We talked about what we would say to Kelly if we could talk to her.

Ben said, "I would tell her that if a judge said, 'Kelly, you have to jump out a window,' and she didn't want to and if the judge asked if anybody would, probably nobody would. But I would jump out the window instead of her. I wish I had been there to put out my arms and catch her. I would probably die, but I would catch her and maybe she would break her arm."

Nathanael said, "I'd tell her I wish I could have known her better."

"We did know her! She's our cousin!" Jon protested.

A grasshopper landed on Kelly's stone. The boys grabbed at it, but it jumped and evaded their clutches. They forgot where we were and why we had come. They fled in hot pursuit of the grasshopper. I let them be. I figured Kelly would be pleased her cousins were having an adventure at her grave. The sun was beginning to burn through the haze. Clouds hung over the mountains. The sunlight glinted off the dew on the grass. Jon took a halting leap. He almost got it. Nathanael and Ben were right behind him, backing him up. Three boys kneeled and lurched in concert, moving forward, backward, to the side, helping each other, focused on the chase. I seemed to hear Kelly laughing from heaven. I think she was rooting for the grasshopper.

❄ ❄ ❄

I was preparing dinner not long ago and thought about James Harrison. He was that newborn baby I had gone to care for when Kelly fell. Now it was his fourteenth birthday. *Has it really been fourteen years? Has Kelly been gone that long?*

My sister's and my "Proud Mary" days are long over—though recently, in a Karaoke café, we pulled off an animated rendition of the Monkees' "Daydream Believer," which was well received. Carol gave birth to two more beauti-

ful daughters. She has probably lost count of the number of
pink toothbrushes that have come and gone in that bathroom.

Six years after Kelly died, my family and I spent two weeks
in the same condo where she fell. It is beautifully located by
Lake Lure, outside of Asheville, surrounded by mountains
with a stream out back. It was filled with the sounds and
smells of summer, the steady gurgling of the stream washing
over stones, warm breezes, and the smell of mown grass. It
was peaceful there. It felt safe. But the first thing I did when
I got there was to go and stand on the concrete patio where
Kelly fell. I had to come to terms with that window. I could
not get over how short a distance she fell. How could it have
killed her? It should only have broken an arm.

I wondered at the faith my sister owned that day on the
swing set when I read those simple words from that little
yellow booklet so many years ago. The Fact-Faith-Feeling
train had somehow kept her on the track. There were
moments it slowed, even stalled. But the train, it turned out,
was bigger than her ability to stop it. It pushed on, and in
time it picked up steam and brought her along with it. What
God did through Jesus is the engine that drives the train. It
pulls the feelings along behind. The engine is too big and
mighty for the caboose to have a chance at driving it.

I think about the Fact-Faith-Feeling train one week out
of every year. That week, my thoughts take me back to a
Carolina summer when the cicadas underscored the Jesus
song we sang when we stood beside a little white casket. One
four-day time span every year we revisit the week our little

Kelly fell, then died, then had a birthday, and then was buried.

Sometimes, living in a world where lawns are mowed and the mail gets delivered, it is easy to forget what's real. In such a world little girls don't die and have to be buried in Easter dresses. Sometimes we get fooled into thinking we own this life. But we don't.

Carol needed me that summer of 1987. I helped her. That, strangely, was Kelly's gift to me. All those years of our childhood and adolescence I was the one who needed Carol. I needed her when we played in the field and at the big log. I needed her in Latin class and when I took her to the swing set to read her *The Four Spiritual Laws*. When we gravitated into other spheres as adults, I lost part of myself. I didn't know where I was. Kelly helped us with that. She showed us the way back. She helped us to understand how to think about life, and death, and the Fact-Faith-Feeling train. And about being sisters. Not a proportionate trade-off, I am well aware, but it's something. It's a reason to put one foot in front of the other and go out and check the mail.

I still look at the picture of Kelly sitting on the stone step, smelling a daffodil, looking up at us with shining eyes and winsome smile. In those moments, my soul comes back to me.

PART TWO

THE UNIVERSE ON FOURTH AND BIRCH

5 *This Is My Body*

When you move into a small town like Barney Ridge* and your husband is the pastor of the Baptist church on the corner, and when your home is right next to the church, you learn quickly that people who are looking for answers about God's mysterious ways frequently begin their search at the pastor's front door—and he's usually not home. That means the search often begins with me, his wife.

Barney Ridge, or Barney, as we came to call it, is a small Roman Catholic town along the northern New Jersey shore that got snagged somewhere between the 1950s and the 1970s without a trace of the 1960s. Five Protestant churches vied for their corners of the Barney Ridge universe, and my husband tended the flock in the universe on the corner of Fourth and Birch. We lived in Barney in the late 1980s.

---

*Names of people, places, and minor details of events in this section (chapters 5 through 8) have been changed to protect the privacy of those involved.

On the appropriate holidays you could walk the streets of our neighborhood and find an American flag draped from every front porch, thanks to Mr. Patterson, who monitored Birch Avenue for such purposes. Victorian homes with wraparound porches and geranium-filled window boxes lined the shady streets that converged at our corner. Our church was up the street from the public library, down the street from the historical society, and a stone's throw away from the old-folks home where Mr. Patterson lived. It stood catty-cornered to the Presbyterians. Every Christmas our deaconesses and theirs engaged in a healthy competition to see which church would be the first to hang the Christmas wreaths on the front doors.

Within the first week after my husband, Bob, and I arrived, we paid a visit to another minister and his wife. Their manse, like our parsonage, was next to the church. Our worlds related in symbiotic juxtaposition, so we thought, and we wanted to get to know these people. We were all smiles when we mounted their front porch that first time. Bob knocked on the front door, and we waited. The curtains were drawn, and we couldn't see in. He knocked again, finally concluding that no one was home. Just as we turned to leave, the door opened behind us. A woman peered out furtively.

"We're new in the neighborhood," Bob said, regaining his stance outside the door. "I'm the new pastor over at the Baptist church. This is my wife, Wendy."

"What?" Her voice cracked.

"Wendy. My name's Wendy," I said.

She told us her name. That was all she said.

"Just wanted to say hello," I said, opting not to set a date to do lunch.

In the course of time I understood why that pastor's wife fortressed herself in a solitary world inside that dark house. After that, I thought of her as the Woman behind the Door.

Barney Baptist was our first church. I did not understand how churches worked, nor did I perceive the nuances behind being married to the pastor of a small church in a small town. Signs of trouble began our first Christmas there when, at the climax of the church's Christmas program Ben Witherington appeared as Santa Claus. Santa came to the front of the church and called my husband and me up to stand with him. He slipped his arm around my waist, and said, "Ho-ho-ho! Here's what Santa has for this good boy and girl." That was how the church presented Bob with his Christmas bonus that year. Their generosity almost made up for the humiliation.

When the issue arose the following year, I objected to Santa's presence, arguing that he belonged in the mall, not in church. Most people took it well and understood my point. A few, whom I will hereafter refer to as the "Santa Revolt Contingent" (SRC), objected. One among them insisted that if there's no Santa, then there shouldn't be any Christmas decorations in the church either, which I never said. The SRC was particularly robust, and if they said there would be no Christmas decorations, there wouldn't be any. The Sunday school classes had always sponsored the church Christmas tree. That year they did not put up a tree.

To compensate, some in the SRC placed in the front of

the sanctuary a four-foot plastic nativity scene with a pink Mary and blue Joseph that lit up when you plugged them in. They did so without consulting the deacons, trustees, my husband, or anyone else. They saw to it that Mary and Joseph's lights were turned on before every Sunday service during Advent.

We weathered that one, but it was touch and go for a while. In time, Bob found his stride, and things began to look up. He possessed a disarming pastoral style, and his jokes from the pulpit on Sunday mornings kept the congregation in stitches. He hugged nearly everyone who came through the receiving line after church, which especially endeared him to the elderly ladies.

One of my favorites was Ina Billingsly, a nervous widow who had white puffy hair, penciled-in eyebrows like McDonald's arches above the brow line, and bright red lips that looked like cherry tomatoes. When she talked, she strung her sentences together with *mmm*s. She was pushing up her teeth, which slipped a lot. She fretted like Aunt Pittypat in *Gone With the Wind*. She told me once she was sure she had contracted AIDS from her nephew, whom she thought was gay but for which she had no real evidence, because he had kissed her on the cheek at a family wedding. She said she hadn't felt well since.

Adelaide Byrd, whom we called Addie, was another favorite, a plain woman who always wore the same pea green overcoat to church, with white ankle socks and black shoes with laces. She had stringy black hair and odd-shaped moles and no thumbs. When she smiled, her eyes curled like half moons. You couldn't help but take to her when she smiled.

In a single two-minute conversation, she could twaddle on about the Huguenots, her husband's big-band tapes, the cat she's allergic to, and the trouble in Israel.

Julie Munson was a younger version of these older ladies, but she was no less enamored with my husband's winning repartee. Now and then Bob dropped by her house and brought her boys over to play with our young sons. He felt sorry for her because she had no control over those boys; they drove her crazy, and Bob thought she could use the break. Julie Munson appreciated these helpful inclinations.

The women of our church found hope and spiritual anchoring in my husband's role as their pastor. They told him their stories, and he listened and sympathized. They drank in his words that spilled from the pulpit on Sunday mornings and always had someone to call when they felt lonely or discouraged. Ina, Addie, Julie, and, in time, most everyone in the church, won my husband's sympathetic ear. As for me, the Santa Revolt served as a foretaste of the complicated and tenuous existence that belonged to the one who happens to be married to everyone else's pastor.

One spring day about halfway through our four-year tenure at Barney Ridge, the issue of peoples' expectations came into clear focus for me. I hadn't slept well the night before, and of all the times for this to have happened, this day was particularly onerous. A business meeting was scheduled for that evening, and I had the task of presenting the case, on behalf of our newly formed missions committee, for increasing the missions budget. Our proposal recommended giving systematic monthly support to four missionary families serving overseas who had some connection to our church. Regular giving meant creating a line in the budget. Things always got messy at church business meetings when we talked about lines and budgets.

The day began inconspicuously. Our two older sons, Nathanael, then eight, whom we called "Than" at the time, and Benjamin, six, were at school. Our youngest son, Jon, then four, spent the morning quietly drawing pictures of monsters, walking fish, and a growling, sharp-toothed "flying slime tongue" in greens, browns, and blacks. He told me to put the slime tongue on the front door "to scare the elephants," which was fine by me. No elephants bothered us for weeks.

Later that afternoon when Jon had gone off to kindergarten, I took the opportunity to catch a nap. I curled up in my bed, positioned the pillows under and over my head, and entered twilight. Then the phone rang. That would be for Bob. And Bob wasn't there. I was tired. I didn't want to answer it. I tried to let it ring, but guilt is a gift that just keeps on giving.

"Hello?"

"Mmm, Wendy?"

The *mmm*s told me it was Ina.

"This is, mmm, Ina. Oh, Wendy," she said, "I'm in such pain! You can't, mmm, believe the pain I'm in."

"What's wrong, Ina?"

"My vagina is burning so bad. I can't get relief. Would you pray for me, Wendy?"

I have prayed for many things and seen some miraculous

answers to prayer. But I had never prayed for anyone's vagina before. I was glad Bob wasn't there to take the call. I asked the Lord to give me the words, and I prayed, over the phone, for Ina's request. It settled her. She thought she could rest after that.

I took the phone off the hook and returned to twilight sleep. That's when the doorbell rang—and rang again.

Jon's flying slime tongue had no effect on Addie Byrd. She stood outside the front door holding a scrapbook under her arm.

"Do you want to do something relaxing?" Her eyes curled.

I almost said I *had* been doing something relaxing, but what was the point?

"There's more light in here," she said, leading me into my kitchen. She indicated where I should sit at my kitchen table and then opened her scrapbook. I angled my head and sometimes pulled the book closer for a better view. She resisted when I did this; she wanted to retain control of the page turning. The book was filled with pencil sketches she had drawn of every town, every hotel room, every cobblestone, and every cloud configuration during a recent trip to England. There were no photographs.

She flipped through the pages gracefully, despite having no thumbs. In her singsongy, high-pitched voice she described "the Wash" and "Cambridgeshire" and points west and east. Every page rendered a surprising detail, like the cloud that looked like a sheep or the pull chain next to the commode. She included the floor plan of each hotel room down to the angle of the study lamp by the bed and every step on every staircase inside every building. The people in her drawings had little balloons over their heads: "Susie and Tim are planning a daisy and clover wedding."

I asked her three times when she had gone to England. She didn't answer. We were lost in a forty-five-minute nonstop linear narrative that, I had to admit, *was* relaxing. After nearly an hour I finally cut her off. I had done this before, and she didn't mind. I thanked her for showing me her pictures and asked if she might draw me a picture of the parsonage. She looked at me and smiled and said okay. Then, within a minute, her countenance dropped. She said her head hurt, and she was awfully busy, and don't I have a picture of it already?

I put on a pot of coffee.

Later that day the vacuum cleaner broke, which wouldn't have been so bad except that it was the church's and Bob got angry at me for breaking it. I told him I wouldn't have been using it at all if our own vacuum cleaner hadn't broken first and if he hadn't concluded there was no sense in buying another one when the church's was right next door. So now we had two broken vacuum cleaners and no money to fix either one.

"Why do they have to make things so cheap?" he said, pounding and yanking in an attempt to fix it. "That's what you get when you buy a cheap machine."

Bob grunted and hissed and pounded a little bit more. He loosened something with a screwdriver and, like a miracle, got the thing to work. He then proceeded to do the vacuuming himself and in the process pulled the cord so that it knocked over the pencil holder on the kitchen counter. Crayons, pencils, pens, scissors, paper clips, and a Spider Man eraser spilled onto the kitchen floor. I felt as if it were my fault. I picked everything up and moved the cord so it wouldn't happen again.

"I'll do this," I said.

He shut it off, put his tools away, and walked out the back door, heading for the church. I finished the vacuuming and swore that if one more person came up that walk, I'd hide behind my couch on my hands and knees before I'd open the front door.

The boys returned home from school, and I marched them right over to the church for Kids Praise choir rehearsal. The children's spring concert was coming up in June, and preparations were already well underway. I had volunteered to provide apple juice and Skittles—"singing pills"—for the practices. As I left the church and made my way back to the parsonage, I noticed a pickup truck parked alongside the curb in front. I couldn't avoid being seen by whoever it was since he was looking at me, so I approached the truck.

It was Ernie Purdle, the father of two church members, Will and Deeter Purdle. Ernie was also an ex-Gideon, a former deacon of our church, and the man who created a town and church scandal a few years before when he left his wife of twenty-five years for another woman.

He rolled down the driver's side window.

"You know me?" he said.

"I think I do."

"Mind if I talk with you a bit?"

He stepped out of his truck and easily stood a foot taller than me. He was gray and balding, and his blue jeans hung low. We sat on the front steps of the parsonage.

"You a minister? You know, an official minister?"

"I get more unannounced visitors here at the house than he gets at the church. I suppose that gives me qualifications as some kind of minister, wouldn't you think?"

"It ain't right for a woman to be a minister. A woman ain't supposed to be a leader in church or have authority over a man. That's in the Bible."

"It's also in the Bible that a woman taught a man."

"Where does it say that?"

"Priscilla 'explained the way of God more adequately' to Apollos, who was 'a learned man with a thorough knowledge of the Scriptures,' Acts chapter 18. And Phoebe was a deacon. That's in Romans 16. I won't bring up Deborah—or Huldah."

"Where'd you learn the Bible like that?"

There was nothing to be gained by telling him I had studied at seminary like my husband. "Is a woman not supposed to know the Bible either?"

This brought the conversation to a temporary impasse. He locked his hands and rolled his thumbs around and fiddled with his baseball cap.

"You know, my boys won't have nothin' to do with my wife. No doubt you heard about all that?"

I nodded.

"She ain't a bad person. People don't know this, but we were in France one time, and she saw a homeless lady walkin' down the street who didn't have no shoes. She took off her shoes, right there in the middle of Paris, France, and gave them to her." He paused.

I broke the silence. "I guess nothing good can come out of a situation like that."

He tilted his head and looked at me. "Would you talk to my boys about it? They like you." His "boys" were both in their late thirties and were deacons in the church.

"Why don't you talk to them about it?"

He pushed himself to a standing position and shoved his hands into the pockets of his jeans. "Well," he said, "I'll be going." He tipped his baseball cap.

I walked with him to his truck. He got in and rolled down the window. "I hear your husband's a good preacher. I'd like to hear him sometime."

"You'd be welcome anytime," I said.

He rolled up his window and pulled away.

By this point I had one hour left in the day to put together the missions proposal for the business meeting. I titled it: "A Biblical Basis for Monthly Financial Support of Missionary Families." For the past several decades, I began, our church's record of missions giving has been sporadic and unreliable. The few missionaries to whom we have rendered financial support have received it in the form of "love offerings" taken once or twice a year at random intervals in varying amounts. The missions committee, I wrote, was therefore proposing that our church adopt a system of consistent and regulated giving "so that these good people can know what is coming from us, and when."

I defended my proposal with "the biblical mandate" citing first Mary (Magdalene), Joanna, Susanna, and others, "who were contributing from their own resources to support Jesus and his disciples." The second example came from the apostle Paul, who received financial support from the church in Philippi: "You Philippians were the only ones who gave me financial help when I brought you the Good News and then traveled on from Macedonia. No other church did this." Beyond Paul and Jesus, I appealed to the model in the book of Acts, when believers bore one another's financial burdens: "They sold their possessions and shared the proceeds with those in need."

I went on to say that according to the Bible, God means for the church to be forward-looking and forward-moving, active and engaged in the world, spreading the good news about the saving work of Christ and bringing cups of cold water to those in physical need. Jesus told his disciples to "go and make disciples of all the nations" and to "teach these new disciples to obey all the commands I have given you." I made a special point of emphasizing that these were the last words Jesus spoke, as documented in Matthew's Gospel.

Our missionaries are addressing the physical needs of the world around them, I said, and it goes without saying that the apostle Paul, not to mention Peter, James, John, and all the twelve disciples and any number of subsequent apostles, gave up their lives and livelihoods for the purpose of going into the "outermost parts" of the then-known world with the message of the gospel.

Therefore, I concluded, it is incumbent upon those of us

who have derived the gracious benefits of God's abundant
bounty to share our earthly resources with those who have
answered that call. We, the missions committee, believe that
God will truly bless us once we take this step of faith and
show ourselves to be outward-looking and self-sacrificing
with our financial giving.

The proposed allotments came somewhere in the vicinity
of fifty dollars a month for four missionary families, totaling
financial support that came to about eighteen hundred
dollars a year. I had worked hard on the proposal and felt I
was ready to present it at the business meeting.

The meeting that evening went breezing along at a friendly
clip in the early going. Should we buy a copier? How much
are we willing to pay to have the nursery carpeted? Should we
get the exterior shingles on the east wall replaced?

It took an unpleasant turn, however, when someone whom
I'll identify only as having been numbered among the SRC,
stood and publicly challenged my husband's and my use of
the baby-sitting allotment. This was a small account the
church had set aside to help offset the cost of baby-sitters
when we both were away on church business.

"It was my understanding," this person said, "that this
money was to be used only when the pastor and Wendy both
had to be away from their children on *church* business,"
implying that we were living a secret life on our eleven-
thousand-dollar-a-year salary and bilking the baby-sitting
fund to take a walk on the wild side.

Bob stood up.

"I'd like to note for the official record that Wendy and I

make use of the baby-sitting money only when it involves church business. Does anyone want to know how we've used this fund during this past quarter?"

No one wanted to know.

That set the tone for the rest of the meeting.

Dewey Hansen, the church clerk and moderator of the meeting, then announced the budget committee had turned down the missions committee's request for monthly support of the missionaries, so there would be no point in my making the presentation. I looked at Jenny Little, our cochair, who was sitting behind me. Her face was so red I thought she had broken out in hives.

She raised her hand. "I'd like to call for a vote from the floor."

This prompted a protracted discussion about whether or not Jenny Little could call for a vote from the floor. Richie Langley, a deacon, pulled *Robert's Rules of Order* off the shelf. He read aloud the section that verified she could. A vote from the floor by a show of hands was begrudgingly taken, and the line on the budget for monthly support of the missionaries passed 43 to 36.

"Who does this missions committee think they are?" and "What have they ever done for the church?" asked a member of the Revolt contingent. Moderator Dewey Hansen, who sympathized, decided the vote didn't count. I objected. I asked Richie to hand me *Robert's Rules of Order.* I proceeded to read where it said the vote did count.

Dewey countered that a quorum wasn't present at the meeting, so it didn't count. I referred again to *Roberts,* which said that in the event there was no quorum—which we never had at church business meetings—the majority wins the vote. Dewey decided to take another vote regardless of what *Robert's Rules* said. But before that happened, the opposition mounted a vigorous verbal assault on the notion of giving away "the church's money" when the furnace didn't work right and the roof in the Sunday school wing had a leak in it.

Out of sheer exasperation Bob insisted we take a second vote and be done with it, whatever the outcome. The majority again voted to support the missionaries, and on any other day I would have been gratified that most of the people at that meeting deemed regular monthly support for missionaries a good thing. But I wasn't rested. What little rest I tried to steal for myself was interrupted by a burning vagina, pencil sketches of every cobblestone in Cambridgeshire, two broken vacuum cleaners, and the town's scandalizer lecturing me about the role of women in the church. I had worked hard on the presentation of the biblical mandate for supporting mission-aries, and the accusation of misuse of the baby-sitting money hadn't helped. So instead of seeing that hard-won victory for the missionaries as a healthy exercise of congregational self-government, I felt annoyed. I mumbled to myself something like, "It's no wonder our building looks as if it was put together by drunken carpenters on a weekend."

At the time I didn't expect anyone would have, or could have, heard me. But I got the sense that some might have. Dewey Hansen abruptly ended the meeting, and Richie Langley seconded. There was no further discussion.

I left alone, in silence, making my escape out the side

door. Addie Byrd intercepted me. "My family thinks I'm insane," she said.

I stopped.

She looked at me. "I told them I wasn't. I told them there are only two things I can't do—throw a ball overhand and climb a rope with knots."

I looked at her and didn't know whether to laugh or cry. Then I said, "I can't climb a rope with knots either."

Later that night the following discussion between Bob and me ensued:

"Are you mad?"

"What would I have to be mad about?"

Silence.

"I don't know why I said it. They got to me."

He looked at me. "Is there anyone who *doesn't* get to you?"

"I didn't come into this church trying to make everybody mad like this."

"Somehow that tends to be the prevailing sentiment you pull out of people. I'm sure it will get back to us in one form or another."

Silence.

"Have you ever thought of just loving these people? Love goes a long way, you know."

"Don't you think interrupting a nap, after a night I hadn't slept, to answer the phone that would no doubt be for you in order to pray for the church hypochondriac, isn't love? I could have referred that one to you."

He didn't respond.

"You don't think it's love to have Addie Byrd at my

kitchen table listening to her one-hour monologue about the Wash? Or sitting with Ernie Purdle on my own front steps while he lectures me about women? I take the Kids Praise choir Skittles for singing pills! Isn't *that* love?"

"I'm not going to talk to you if you start yelling."

"I'm not yelling."

Silence.

"What do you want me to do, stand up in the pulpit and tell everybody to leave my wife alone?"

"Yes!"

"I can't do that. You know that."

Silence.

"What do you expect? These are fallen sinful people, just like you. Just like me." He hesitated. "Did you forget? You won the vote. You won."

✳ ✳ ✳

I finished the vacuuming the following day. Bob was away with a deacon on a golf outing. The boys were at school. I was alone. I was winding the cord to the vacuum cleaner, preparing to return it to the church, when I looked out my window and saw Addie Byrd shuffling up our front walk. I froze. I looked again. She was climbing the front steps. I experienced a moment of panic and indecision. Then I darted behind the couch, kneeling on my hands and knees. She rang the bell. I was on all fours, breathing heavily, my head lowered. I felt sure she saw me, but I didn't care. She rang the bell a second time. *Even if she sees me,* I thought, *I'm not answering that door.* It felt like a torturously long time before I heard something drop on the porch, followed by the sound of Addie's feet shuffling away. I raised my head and saw her clutching the strap of her little black purse with her four fingers and ambling down the front walk. She was halfway up the block before I stood up.

I was sweeping the front porch a few days later and found a small package behind the planter box. That's when I remembered Addie Byrd and the day she visited and dropped something on the porch, the day I hid behind the couch. Inside a plastic bag I found drawing paper and colored pencils and a note that read: "For Nathanael, Ben, and Christopher. From Byrd." She never could remember Jon's name. At the bottom of the bag I found a dollar bill paper-clipped to a note. "For the missionaries," it said.

How had I gotten to the place where I'd hide on my hands and knees behind my couch before answering my front door? *Who am I? What is my place in this network of relationships?*

I was becoming increasingly isolated, made worse, in my mind, by the fact that I had also become my husband's antagonist. I was the source of his problems, or so it seemed. It started with the Santa revolt and was exacerbated by the missions-giving battle. Trying to explain myself only made me feel more isolated. Couldn't he see I was trying my hardest to "love these people"?

A person told me one time that I didn't act like a pastor's wife. I asked her how a pastor's wife acts. She said, "The one I know just stands there with a blank expression on her face." I know that look. Sometimes when a pastor's wife hears her husband's prophetic word on Sunday mornings, it gets lost in the fog of the fight from the night before, when he got mad because she left the bathroom light on. She's heard all the jokes before and can't relate to the amens and hallelujahs. Of course she can't say this to anybody. Who would she tell? The Ladies Aid society? Who does she call? She doesn't have a pastor. Sometimes standing there with a blank expression on her face is all she's got.

Jesus scandalized church people with all his touching and hobnobbing with women and prostitutes and other ignominious ne'er-do-wells. I would fantasize about how he told the woman with the menstrual hemorrhage, "Daughter, your faith has made you well," and how he raised Jairus's little girl from the dead. I'd close my eyes and picture him taking her hand and calling her back to life and telling the family to get her something to eat. *If only I could hear Jesus say, "Daughter," to me. If only he would take my hand the way he took Jairus's little girl's hand. What would it feel like to hold Jesus' hand? To have him look me in the eye and call me "daughter"? One moment like that would carry me through my lifetime*, I thought.

But Jesus wasn't there to take my hand. I heard no one whispering *daughter* in my ear. The church was Jesus' hands and lips. The church was all I had.

Communion Sunday followed shortly after that business meeting. I found myself confronted with a dilemma. There had been many times during our days at Barney Baptist when I had thought about not participating in the Lord's Supper. The Christmas season with the plastic nativity scene comes immediately to mind. I concluded, however, that if I refrained from Communion every time I felt alienated from someone in the church, I might as well skip the sacrament altogether, which would only have gotten people wondering what sin I was harboring or what person I was mad at. In the end, it would have reflected badly on Bob and caused more problems. So I saw it as a form of personal sacrifice to keep taking the elements (in spite of broken relationships), in deference to a greater good.

"This is the day we celebrate the tradition known as the Lord's Supper," Bob said in preparation. "It was inaugurated by Jesus himself in the upper room on the night our Lord was betrayed, the last night of his life. As we follow his command to keep this tradition alive until his return, let us not come to this table by rote, simply because, as Baptists, Communion is something we do the first Sunday of every month. Let us not partake lightly, thinking we can do so with our lips only and not, in some mysterious way, also with our hearts. Paul tells us to approach the table with soberness of mind, searching our hearts to make sure that we are right with God. If we are not right with him in an inward sense, then we dare not partake of these elements in an outward sense. For if we do, we will eat and drink judgment upon ourselves. We will be hardening our hearts and putting a callused shell between ourselves and the Lord, between his will and our wills. If we continue to harden our hearts and thicken that shell, we will one day come to the point where that shell becomes our tomb," he said.

"My word to you this morning is to soften your hearts. Make your spirit alive toward God. He will come in and make you on the inside what you say you are on the outside. That is his promise. It is his mystery."

The deacons were moving from pew to pew, passing the trays with the little cubes of bread and the little cups of grape juice. Our three boys sat restlessly next to me. The organ started playing, and they knew better than to fuss. This was church, and they were expected to behave and participate, not because they were pastor's kids, but because we were Christians.

I thought about the words from Psalm 55 I had read earlier that morning: "Listen to my prayer, O God, do not ignore my plea; hear me and answer me. My thoughts trouble me and I am distraught. . . . My heart is in anguish within me. . . . I said, 'Oh, that I had the wings of a dove! . . . I would flee far away and stay in the desert.'"

Fleeing wasn't an option. What should I do? Partake and spare further controversy? Revere the words of warning, acknowledge the mystery, and refrain?

I thought of Pop Lundgren, a beloved elderly man in the church. He and his wife, Ermine ("Gram"), had attended since they were newlyweds and had raised their kids in Barney Baptist Sunday school. Their daughter, Lottie, was the woman Ernie Purdle had married and then left for another woman twenty-five years later. Lottie had died shortly after that. The doctors said it was something like cancer, but the general consensus was that Ernie's leaving was what killed her. For eighteen months Pop didn't take Communion because of the bitterness in his heart over what Ernie did to his only daughter.

I visited Pop and Gram every Friday and had told them about the business meeting, how it took a bad turn, how some people might have heard a comment I let slip. Pop said, "When you walk out that door, I want you to tell the Lord to take this burden, that it's too big for you. Just give it to him, and he'll take care of it. And then don't you worry about it no more." Anyone who lived for ninety-two years and could still have that kind of faith was someone I wanted to listen to.

Richie Langley stepped up to our pew. I thought about my call and came to see that "sparing further controversy" wasn't a burden I had the capacity to bear. Sometimes, *not* doing things is the better course, the more positive expression of authentic obedience. In this case, not taking Communion seemed the way to give up the burden, give it to God, and open up the possibility of a movement of the Spirit to fix this mess.

Richie Langley leaned in and lowered the plate in front of me. He didn't flinch when I waved him on and said, "No, thank you."

6 *Pop's Garden*

During the early years when Barney was a one-street town, the Lundgrens bought a piece of land on the hill east of town. Pop kept a garden from which he fed their five children. Every summer Gram put up three hundred containers of corn, cabbage, rhubarb, tomatoes, and anything else Pop harvested. He went door-to-door selling the leftovers and became known as "Farmer Will on Barney Hill." After they learned that Reverend Springer didn't object to the children's wearing dungarees, the Lundgrens walked from the hill to town to attend services at Barney Baptist on Sunday mornings.

Eventually Pop and Gram got too old to handle that much land, and they moved into town. When Pop learned I wanted to put in a garden, he decided to work out his digging impulses in my backyard. Each spring he arrived unannounced, shovel and hoe in hand, and started turning over the earth. It worked out better if I stayed out of the way. One year I "helped" by putting in the row of beans, and they came up crooked. I heard no end of it. Pop had his own way of doing things.

The boys loved Pop and followed him around. I watched him dig up a fat juicy earthworm and dangle it on a finger in front of their faces and then scoop it up like he was dropping it into his mouth. Later that day the boys came in with worms in paper cups and said they wanted to eat them just like Pop did. Another time we had been away at the park, and Pop put a pickle-shaped watermelon he had found at the farmer's market in with my patch of cucumbers. When the boys ran to the garden to see what was ready for picking, they thought they were witnessing a miracle because we had grown a cucumber as big as a watermelon.

That spring, shortly after the business meeting, Pop arrived late on a Saturday morning. He promised to keep the plot little, but Pop's definition of little spanned the length of the backyard. He had been digging about an hour when I went outside to offer him something to drink.

"The ground's dry. There ain't been much rain," he said. Beads of sweat had formed on his brow. The breeze off the bay was blowing his white hair into his face. His eyes were focused on the ground. The shovel sounded like crunching toast when he pressed it into the dirt. "Sometimes the hardest thing to do is to put in a garden when the ground is hard," he said. "You gotta keep turnin' it over. The harvest will come. You gotta believe that."

"You want something to drink, Pop? Lemonade? Soda?"
He always responded the same way. "You got any water?"

I brought him water. He stopped digging and sat on a lawn chair.

"You're looking pale, Pop. You all right?"

"I feel a little dizzy. Maybe I'll sit for a minute."

He sat for a long time. It occurred to me that he must have felt incapable of doing any more but didn't want to leave with the job undone.

"Maybe I'll give it a try," I said. "If I'm ever going to plant a garden on my own, I'm going to have to know how to do this. I'm not always going to have my own personal gardener."

If it had been up to me I would have settled for one third of the surface area Pop had staked out. But I knew sure as he was sitting there, if I had stopped, he would have picked up the shovel and finished the job himself, even if it killed him. My back hurt and my arms were weak, but by God's miraculous provision, I turned over the entire plot.

Pop look satisfied.

"I'll take you home in the car," I said.

He didn't object.

"I just ain't had much of an appetite lately," he said, leaning into the passenger seat.

I shut the door and walked around to the driver's side.

"You need to get more rest. You try to do too much. I'll put the garden in. I promise not to plant the beans crooked."

The following Sunday Gram came to church without Pop.

I sat behind her. "Pop still not feeling well?"

"Oh, he ain't half hisself. Deeter's with 'im, God love 'im." Deeter was son number two of Ernie and Lottie

Purdle, and he was Gram's favorite grandson. (That's why she always said, "God love 'im" after saying his name.) "He came to pick us up for church, and when he saw Pop couldn't barely dress hisself, why Deeter said there ain't no way he was going anywhere. He brought me and then went back home to take him to the doctor."

Later that day, after church, Bob and I went to call on Pop. As usual, we let ourselves in. And, as usual, Gram was settled in her rocker watching Judge Wapner. She clutched a tissue in her left hand because Judge Wapner always made her cry. "The world would be a better place if ever'body was the kind of good man he is."

We both hugged her, and she waved us into the bedroom where Pop was resting. "I'll never hear the end of it if you don't just go on in," she said.

Pop was in his bed. His cotton pajamas hung on him like a shower curtain, and white stubble sprouted from his sunken cheeks. Still, he looked better than he had the last time I saw him, sitting on my lawn chair and sipping the water. He had color, and his eyes were clear.

"Hey, Pop, how you feeling?" I leaned over and gave him a kiss on his cheek.

He lifted his bony hand and took my shoulder. He felt like a skeleton when I put my arms around him. He reached over to shake Bob's hand.

"Reverend, you shoulda seen your wife diggin' her garden," he said. "What kind of man am I to let a woman do that kinda work?"

"I wanted to do it, Pop," I protested.

He rested a minute. "Do you believe angels visit people, Rever'nd?"

"Yes, I do," Bob said.

"I had a dream one time that I was sure was an angel visiting me. It was just before Lottie died. Like they was tellin' me she was going to die. She died the very next day."

"God visits us in ways we don't always understand, Pop. Maybe it was an angel trying to prepare you for her death. Sometimes God comes to us in our dreams."

Pop didn't speak for a few minutes. Judge Wapner was droning in the background, but Pop didn't pay it any mind. He turned his head to face the opened window. A refreshing breeze cut through the stifling stale air of his bedroom. Neighborhood kids were riding Big Wheels on the sidewalk, and the noise set off someone's dog. I took Pop's hand. He looked back toward us.

"Jesus said whatever is bound on earth will be bound in heaven, right Rever'nd? And whatever is loosed on earth will be loosed in heaven. That means we have to forgive in this lifetime, don't it?"

"Jesus wants us to keep short accounts, Pop."

He lifted his eyes to look at Bob. I hadn't realized how icy blue they were. "Have you ever had to forgive anybody, Rever'nd?"

"Lots of times."

"I guess you just do it, whether you feel like it or not."

"If you do the right thing, most of the time the feelings follow." Bob shifted his weight and leaned in, which signaled he was about to tell Pop he was going to pray for him. He cleared his throat.

"You're looking tired, Pop. Why don't you let me pray for you?"

"I wish you would."

I sat on the edge of Pop's bed, holding his hand. Bob stood next to me with one hand on my shoulder and the other on Pop's. Bob asked the Lord to deliver Pop from his pain and thanked him for Pop's friendship and his example of godliness. Bob prayed for Gram, too, and asked the Lord to comfort them both.

What with the dog barking, the kids roaring up and down the street on Big Wheels, and Judge Wapner giving someone the what-for, I found it difficult to concentrate. I opened my eyes. Tears were falling from Pop's face. They were getting caught in his stubble. After the prayer Pop looked up, like he was looking into heaven. He squeezed my hand. "There's only one time I had to forgive somebody," he said.

That would have been Ernie Purdle. After Lottie died and after eighteen months of refraining from Communion, Pop saw Ernie Purdle make an appearance at a church program to watch his grandchildren. If anyone had noticed him, they hadn't shown it. Ernie stood there nervously with his arms folded in front.

Pop walked to his place in the pew. Gram had already settled. At one point he turned and looked back at the door where his ex-son-in-law had been standing. But by then Ernie had bowed out.

Not long after that, Ernie showed up at another program at church. Once again Ernie was standing alone at the back. And, like the last time, the ushers let him be. He stood by himself at the back, curling the program in his palms, look-ing for a place to sit.

Then Pop stood up and left the fourth row. He nudged his way to the end of the pew, and Gram looked at him. He was wearing the same baggy pants and blue button-down sweater with brown stripes that he always wore. He reached the aisle and walked to the back of the sanctuary, where he stopped next to Ernie. Putting one arm on Ernie's back, he shook his hand. Then he pointed in the direction of the fourth pew and led the way back. They took a seat together next to Gram, who nudged over as best she could.

❊ ❊ ❊

My string beans came in straight that year. Pop was right when he said the harvest would come. We learned that Pop's weakness was the result of a cancerous tumor growing inside his stomach. The last time I saw him was a day in the mid-summer. He was lying in his bed and couldn't get water up through the straw when I tried to give him some. I held his hand. It was cold and bony. He hardly had enough strength to lift it.

"You know what I did last night?" he said in a weak voice. "I shoveled and dug and hoed in your garden all night."

A monsoon hit Barney Ridge on a Sunday in July right after church. The sky darkened, and the wind kicked up so fast and furious that no one knew what hit. The rain came hard and water poured down the street like a rushing river. That storm was Pop's escort to heaven. He died at 12:37, just as the clouds turned black and the winds kicked up.

The sanctuary was filled for his funeral. In all our years at that church we had never seen the sanctuary that full. Pop's casket rested at the front of the sanctuary. He looked like the old Pop, ruddy-faced and happy, like the Pop who fooled my boys into thinking he ate worms. Bob preached from Pop's favorite Bible passage, from John's Gospel, where Thomas asked Jesus, "'How can we know the way?' Jesus told him, 'I am the way, the truth, and the life.'"

When the service was over, Gram leveraged herself up onto her walker and hobbled down the aisle, right past the casket, and out the side door. She didn't so much as toss a glance at Pop. People hovered outside on the steps until Deeter and Will and the Lundgren sons carried Pop's casket to the hearse.

Pop picked a beautiful spot for his plot, right under a big oak tree. Deeter and Will were there with their wives, Gram, and her remaining sons. Pop was buried next to Lottie.

Bob read from his little book, "To the thirsty I will give from the fountain of the water of life without payment. He who conquers shall have this heritage, and I will be his God and he shall be my son." We stood under the oak tree next to Pop's grave and sang "The Old Rugged Cross," Pop's favorite hymn. I honestly had never cared for it. It always seemed so *Baptist*. But we sounded good for such a small gathering. The birds sang with us. The sun was shining, and the breeze lifted our skirts so that we had to hold them down. The oak tree covered us in its shade. And I saw, as we stood there singing Pop's hymn, those who had hurt me and whom I had hurt. It was a mystery to think about the movements of God in such people. We were human, and so, failures. But I caught a glimpse of how human failure is where God's movements begin. "Behold, this is our God; We have waited for Him, and he will save us," the prophet Isaiah says. The waiting part is where we tend to forget that our failures do not write the whole script.

Pop showed us that if we wait on God, do right by him, eventually he'll bring us to a new place, a place where we would not go by human inclination. He'll give us the ability to rise up out of a pew and walk to someone who had kept things bound on earth and give us the ability to loose that binding and find a way free. "He who conquers shall have this heritage," and I couldn't help but think that that kind of "conquering" was the heritage Pop was bequeathing to all of us standing there around his simple grave under that oak tree. It doesn't come in dramatic flourishes but in small steps, moving forward, the way Pop did things, like turning over the hard, dry earth one shovelful at a time.

7 *Yellow Pants*

By late summer the Barney Baptist Bombers had made it to the church league softball team play-offs. Despite everyone's dire predictions, the Bombers had begun the season with a flurry of wins, which set the pace for subsequent critical wins, like when they beat arch rivals Red River Baptist, who usually trounced them. You would have thought the Bombers had whooped up on the Yankees with that win. Can-do ebullience mounted with every Barney at bat as the Bombers stacked up runs and later, by the season's end, wins. God was still in his heaven.

After Pop died, things settled down. Everyone at church had loved him and missed him as much as the next person, which, I suppose, put us on equal footing and eliminated the fighting. Anyway, for reasons I still don't understand, after the immediate sense of loss had subsided, coupled with the Bomber wins, peoples' moods changed, and we began to feel as if we were on the same team.

By the fourth of July the Bombers were head-to-head with Red River for the first-place spot. Will Purdle, team captain, was pitcher. Bob played the tenth-man position of short-fielder (not to be confused with shortstop), Richie Langley played left field, Donny Bodine at center, and Deeter Purdle at right. Richie, we came to find out, had a great throwing arm and one time threw out a base runner at home plate after catching the ball at the home-run fence. Donny Bodine managed to keep his name on the church membership roll because he made it out to pancake breakfasts now and then. He hit behind Bob and ran so fast that it was all Bob could do to keep Donny from lapping him when they ran the bases. Bob was forever huffing and puffing with Donny Bodine hitting behind him.

Since I had expressed an interest, Will designated me the official team scorekeeper. He gave me a brief and disorienting tutorial, then left it up to me to decide what was a hit and what was an error. Early on, Bob helped me figure it out, and I quickly reached the point where I felt confident making the calls myself, even with the Bombers looking over my shoulder at the scorebook to see how I had scored their most recent at bat.

The Bombers made it to the pennant play-off, the game that would determine who would advance to the championship final that summer. They faced the defending champs, Red River Baptist. The pennant game was held on a Monday evening. The skies were clear but hazy, and the humidity was so thick that the players' polyester uniforms stuck to them like fly paper and their sweat left salty white ridges on the brows of their caps. We hadn't won every game that season, but we won more than any of the other teams except Red River. Our records were tied coming into that final game. The Bombers were tagged as the underdogs.

Red River's captain was a man named Nickie. What he lacked in pomposity, he made up for in boorishness. I walked over to Red River's bench to get their lineup, as scorekeepers are obliged to do, and he bellowed to Will Purdle within earshot of both teams, "I thought pastors' wives were supposed to play the organ!" He handed me their scorebook with the lineup and said, "You know the difference between a strikeout and a base on balls, honey?" Nickie strutted around the backstop, checking out the baselines and yucking it up with the umpire. He winked at me when I asked him not to call me honey.

Because this was a church league, some players' uniforms were ragtag leftovers from previous seasons. Some jerseys didn't have numbers, and others didn't match their team's colors. This could be a scourge on score keeping because in addition to keeping track of hits, runs, and fielding plays, the scorekeeper also kept track of the batting order, which is where the numbers on the jerseys came into play.

So I concocted my own system for keeping track of the other team's batting order. Writing their names and numbers wasn't all that helpful, given the fact that some players didn't have numbers, and depending on whether they batted right-handed or left-handed, you might not see their numbers anyway. With each team member's first at bat I'd include an additional identifying feature. For example, if

Jenkins, number 12, was the leadoff batter, I would also write—in the case of Red River's leadoff batter—Bushy Beard. The number-two batter—Williams, number 24—was Black Guy. Batter number three was Armpit Hole. Red River's cleanup hitter, fourth in the batting order, didn't have a proper uniform. He was Yellow Pants.

Success in score keeping stands or falls on the ability not to become distracted by chitchat. Most spectators don't pay attention to the game unless there is a come-from-behind rally or a debacle. Most people sit and gab, talking about their day at the beach or the visit to the dentist. They lose track of the game and then, when the inclination strikes, turn to the scorekeeper to bring them up to speed. Admittedly it is a pleasant feeling to be looked upon as the go-to person, and it would have been tempting to give in to the desire to please. But the consequences for score keeping can be disastrous.

Documenting every fielding play can be complicated, especially when after each player's at bat, he looks over your shoulder at the scorebook, checking to see whether you credited him with a hit or an error. Do you know what a fielder's choice is? Do you know when to put down a forward K or a backward K (for a strikeout and a strikeout swinging, respectively)? Do you know what a 6-4-3 play is? The scorekeeper is expected to know these things. If the batter hits a grounder that gets scooped up by the shortstop, who tosses it to the second baseman, who rifles it to the first baseman, it gets scored 6-4-3 DP—double play (2 outs)—and you'd better get it right.

Every strike, hit, fielding play, run, and out, gets written in the scorebook, and sometimes all of the above happens in a single flourish. At the same time, you're keeping track of the batting order, which is why the scorekeeper gets the list from the opposing team captain before the first at bat. The batting order must be maintained throughout the game unless the umpire and opposing team are notified of a change and the change is recorded in the scorebook.

Everyone expected Barney Baptist to get pummeled. Bob, number 10, was nimble in his position as shortfielder and possessed an uncanny ability to get on base. He seemed to provide the spark that ignited the rest of the team members. Their bats came alive, and their defense was taut and disciplined. There were surprising moments when they actually looked like baseball players.

As this was the pennant game, the crowd was unusually engaged, and there were few distracting interruptions for the scorekeeper. Ben and Jon, our younger sons, played on the jungle gym and swing set with the other kids, and Than served as the team batboy and helped me keep track of scoring.

The Bombers struggled through the first three innings. We were behind 4 to 1 when, at the bottom of the third, Red River's Bushy Beard got up and hit a home run with two men on. That ballooned the score to 7 to 1 at the top of the fourth.

The bottom of the fourth brought Bomber Donny Bodine up to bat. He swung at the first pitch and rifled it over the head of Red River's shortstop, and it fell in the gap between second and third. Only Donny B could have stretched that into a double, he was that fast. Then Will Purdle was up. He fancied himself a home-run hitter but usually ended up popping up. Deeter yelled from the bench, "Don't be no hero! Just get on base!" Will took his time and waited for his pitch. The count was two strikes, two balls when the right pitch came, and he leveled his swing and landed the ball inside the first-base line. Donny Bodine ran home, and Will safely made it to first, 7 to 2. Richie Langley was up in the cleanup spot. He swung like he was aiming for the moon and missed the ball, but he pulled his back and stepped out of the batter's box in pain.

"Shake it off, Richie. We need a hit."

He stretched his back, both arms straight up, holding the bat, then stepped back into the batter's box.

"What's the score?" I heard from behind.

"2 to 7, them."

"Poke it through, Richie. Just get on base."

The pitch came in, and Richie missed the moon a second time. But he knicked the ball and it bobbled foul, which fooled the Red River catcher, who didn't go after it. Then it rolled fair. Richie made it to first; Will made it to second; no outs.

That began a rally that landed the Bombers in the lead, 12 to 7, by the end of the fourth inning. Softball games can turn around just like that. The Bombers didn't let the lead make them overconfident. The Red River hitters sauntered up to bat, cocksure as ever.

Church league games go seven innings. At the bottom of the sixth, Red River's Jelly Belly hit a home run, making it 12 to 8. Heart Tattoo, the pitcher, struck out. Bushy Beard and Black Guy each got on base with one-out singles.

Before Will lofted each pitch, he looked around to make sure the fielders were where he wanted them. Now and then he signaled for someone to move to the left, or he'd wave for the outfielders to back up if the batter was a slugger.

"Down the middle, Will, let's go!" Bob said from short field.

"Come on, Will, strike this guy out!"

He arced it high but caught the strike zone on its descent. The batter, Armpit Hole, looked at it. The next pitch was way outside. Will took his cap off and wiped his brow. One out with two people on. Armpit Hole wanted it. If he could get a base hit, at least one of the base runners would score. If he could hit a home run, it would bring them within one run of tying.

Will's next pitch was high, but Armpit Hole was fooled. He chased it. Strike Two.

"One more, Will! You can get this guy!"

"He'll swing at anything! You can do it, Will!"

Will checked the outfield. Richie, in left, was where he wanted him. He pulled Deeter in a few steps at right. Donny Bodine, in center, was ready.

The ball hit the plate coming in. Ball two.

The next pitch came in. Armpit Hole was ready for it and found the sweet spot. He launched it out of the park. Just like that, the score was 12 to 11.

Will managed to finish the inning without anyone else scoring, but Red River was right back in it. The Bombers were rattled.

Bob was the first one up at the top of the seventh inning.

Uncharacteristically he swung at the first pitch and blooped it behind the third baseman and made it safely to first. Donny B batted behind him and bunted—not for any strategic reason other than the element of surprise. It worked. Only Donny Bodine was fast enough to make it to first base without a throw on a bunt. Will struck out trying to be the hero. Richie Langley popped out, but the sacrifice got Bob and Donny home. Two outs, 14 to 11. Deeter was up. He took two pitches, both strikes, and then hit it down the first-base line. Unfortunately he tried to stretch his hit into a double and got thrown out at second. We were up by three at the bottom of the last inning when Red River was up. They were at the bottom of their batting order. There was a chance we could hold them off.

Before the Bombers ran onto the field, they grabbed their gloves and gathered in a circle at the bench. "We gotta hold 'em," Will said. "Infield, stay tight. Don't let anything by. Richie, be ready to make the throw at the plate if they make it to the top of their order."

"It ain't gonna get that far, Will," said Donny. "We're gonna end it right here."

"Let's go!"

They fanned out to their positions. Will stood on the mound and righted his cap. He arced the pitch too high and walked the first batter, Fat Butt.

The next two were easy outs. Jelly Belly struck out swinging, and their pitcher, Heart Tattoo, struck out looking.

Fat Butt was on first base with two outs. Bushy Beard, the top of their order, got up. Will walked him.

"Get the next guy, Will. Come on. Let's go. One more out."

Fat Butt and Bushy Beard were on first and second. Black Guy reached for an outside pitch, which would have been a ball, but the ball caught the end of the bat. He blooped into shallow right. Deeter charged the ball and got it to the second baseman, but by that time the bases were loaded. The score was 14 to 11. A home run could win it, and Red River could steal the pennant.

Yellow Pants stepped into the batter's box.

Sweat poured from Will's face. The infielders crouched and pounded their gloves, ready to snatch anything that came anywhere close. The outfielders looked at each other and waved each other in or out, depending on their positions.

"Come on, Will, one more out! This is your moment! You can do it!" his wife, Lucy, cried from the stands.

Will threw the pitch high. Ball one. Yellow Pants backed off and stepped out of the batter's box.

"What's the score?"

"14 to 11, us."

I checked the scorebook to see who Will would be facing if Yellow Pants got on base and a run or two scored.

Yellow Pants wiggled his hips and dug in his feet, poised for the next pitch.

Where was Armpit Hole? He was supposed to be up after Black Guy. Yellow Pants was supposed to hit after Armpit Hole. I looked at their bench. Armpit Hole was yucking it up with Yankees Hat, who was putting on his batting gloves.

I called Than. He was fastidious about details.

"Isn't Armpit Hole supposed to be up?"

Will threw the next pitch. Yellow Pants swung and missed. One ball. One strike.

"Who's Armpit Hole?" he asked.

"Over there. That guy, right there. Wasn't he supposed to bat next?"

"You better say something," said Than.

I had never encountered a batting-order violation. I wasn't sure what the protocol was. Do you interrupt the game? Do you walk up to the plate? This much I knew. If I didn't do something, no one else would. Only the score-keeper kept track of these kinds of details.

Will had already thrown two pitches. If Yellow Pants landed one before I pointed out the violation, it would be too late. The violation counts only if someone calls them on it.

"Excuse me." I stood up. "Sorry, I hate to interrupt," I said, walking toward the umpire, waving my pencil. "I think he's the wrong batter. This guy who's batting isn't due up yet."

The ump called time. Will put the ball in his glove and his hands on his waist. The rest of the Bombers stood in their positions on the field, all eyes on me. The Red River base runners straightened up, a hush descended on the crowd, and the game came to a standstill. The umpire and I stood in close proximity as I pointed out the violation according to my scorebook.

Nickie ran up from the Red River bench and pulled off his cap.

The umpire took off his mask to get a better look at my book.

Bushy Beard.

Black Guy.

Armpit Hole.

Yellow Pants.

"Armpit Hole?" he said.

"Over there on the bench. This guy here, wearing the yellow pants, is supposed to bat after that guy over there"—I pointed to the bench—"the one with the hole in his armpit. Armpit Hole."

Nickie took my book and cocked his head, confident I had made a mistake in the scoring. He hesitated, scowled, and returned my book. He looked at the ump, threw up his arms, and walked back to the bench.

"He's out!" the ump yelled, meaning Yellow Pants. That ended the game and conferred the pennant, and the right to advance to the championship, to the Barney Baptist Bombers.

The guys exploded in leaps and cheers on the field. The spectators roared. Will ran up to me and planted a kiss on my cheek.

"You won it for us! You're the hero!" he said.

I was swarmed by hugging players.

"She's the hero! The pastor's wife is the hero!"

Funny how things can change, I thought.

Imagine, me—the hero! I wish Pop could have been there. He would have loved this. Pop used to say that when you keep your head up and move forward, things have a way of coming into order and God's will gets done. It made me think of scoring a softball game. The rules of the game are sound. The boundaries are clear and can't be moved. Sometimes

batters strike out swinging; sometimes they strike out looking. Sometimes they find the sweet spot, and what a feeling
that is. The key is knowing the rules, watching the baseline,
keeping your glove soft, refusing to be distracted, and
remembering that even the best batters fail at the plate 70
percent of the time.

8 *The Harvest*

The summer following the Bombers' championship season—
yes, they took the trophy the year Yellow Pants lost the game
for Red River—Bob answered the call to pastor a church in
Honduras, so we left Barney Ridge. I spent the final weeks in
Barney Ridge dismantling our life and squeezing what I
could into ten U-Haul dish-pak boxes. We were allowed to
bring only what we could carry with us on the plane.

Gram cried when I broke the news to her. "I'm glad Pop
ain't here for this," she said. "I've never loved anyone like
you and the Reverend. I think of you as soon as I get up in
the morning."

Once the announcement was made and the people of the
church had had a chance to absorb the shock, that last summer
played out along the lines of its normal themes. The Bombers
fell into a slump and had to relinquish the championship
trophy they had won the previous year. Nonetheless, our final
days were punctuated with exhilarating moments from our

three sons' Little League season. Nathanael played first base on his team and was so consistent at scooping up grounders down the first-base line and making the out that, after a particularly close and crushing defeat, the opposing team's coach gave him the team ball anyway. Ben used to throw his head back and lose his helmet pedaling to first base to beat the throw, while Jon, who played left field, more times than not became distracted looking for bugs or four-leaf clovers. Those final days in Barney Ridge were filled with high fives, water drunk right out of the jug, and bubble-gum chews.

The good will that bubbled forth after I won the pennant for the Bombers extended to the end of our stay. People offered to help me pack. Others propped me up during the house sale. Still others cooked us meals. Many asked whether I was excited about moving overseas, what I hoped it would be like, or if I would miss the mall. I did not know how to respond to these questions. I was consumed with thoughts about where to pack the Legos and what size kennel to buy for the dog and whether I could use laundry detergent instead of upholstery cleaner to clean the couch for the garage sale.

Garage sales, it turned out, were the Barney Baptist women's strong suit. They came over and helped me price everything in my house, right down to the sugar bowl. I would pull out a Pyrex baking dish from the cupboard and ask, "How much for this?"

"Two dollars."

"What about this [a cookbook]?"

"Fifty cents."

The day of the sale itself, the shopping horde started
arriving two hours before the advertised starting time.
People picked through my world, and the church women
held me together. One man took me to task over the price
of the cookbook, and let's just say he caught me at a bad
moment on a hard day. "It has spots on the cover," he said.

"You're not buying it for what's on the cover."

"Twenty-five cents."

"Fifty."

A friend from the church intervened. "Look, mister, she's
moving to Central America. The price is fifty cents." He
passed on the cookbook.

I felt such gratitude for the help of these kind women that
I started giving things to them—my microwave, some of Bob's
sweaters, my wall hanging of the Serenity Prayer.

Ina Billingsley called a day later. She wasn't feeling well,
she said, and she wondered if Pastor Bob could stop by for a
visit. I told her I was sure he would. She said, "You come
along, too, Wendy."

I can't honestly say that I remember what ailment we
prayed about that day. She was happy to see us. She looked
altogether different without her false teeth, arched eyebrows,
and red lips. Her face was sunken, her lips pale, her cheeks
puckered because her teeth weren't in. She asked if she could
hold her cat while we prayed. Bob put his hand on her
shoulder. She stroked her cat with one hand, and I took the
other one. Bob prayed the way he always prayed, the way that
made people cry. She wiped the tears from her cheeks when
he finished. She looked at me, still holding my hand.

"I pray for you every day," she said, her eyes red and moist. "I pray that the burdens of the sick won't wear you down and that the Lord will give you the deepest desires of your heart." Still holding my hand, she looked at Bob and then turned back to me. "He's answered every prayer you prayed for me."

On the way home I said, "I've never seen Ina without her teeth." Other than that, we drove home in silence.

Ina died the next day.

On the Saturday of our last weekend in Barney, I was sitting on our front lawn. Our Labrador puppy squirmed in the clover. The breeze off the bay soothed my throbbing head. I had made a thousand dollars on the garage sale. The parsonage was an empty shell now. Minivans rolled up and down our street, and my familiar world—my home, my grocery store, my garden—was evaporating in front of my eyes. The Legos were packed in the carry-on. The couch sold uncleaned—no time.

Nathanael gave his bike away that day. It had been a present for his ninth birthday. He had picked it out himself and kept it in the garage. He'd wiped it off every day to keep it from rusting. When his friend arrived with his mother to pick it up, Than rolled it out of the garage and handed it over without flinching. Then he heaved it into the trunk of their car. They waved at us and drove off. He came and sat with me on the grass, and we watched our puppy, Bilbo, play.

Addie Byrd shuffled by. She said she wanted to give me something. She was carrying a white paper bag from which she pulled an embroidery hoop, some colored thread, and a piece of folded embroidery cloth. I opened the cloth and saw two hand-drawn images of the parsonage on it. One showed the house angled from the east side, the way it looked when she walked to town on her many trips down our sidewalk. The other was angled from the west, the way it looked walking back home. Underneath she wrote: Beautiful House. Barney Ridge, New Jersey, 1990. She smiled, and her eyes looked like half-moons. She handed it to me, along with a note, and shuffled off, clutching her little black purse with her four fingers.

I opened the note: "We enjoyed your association so much. Speaking of memories, Bob said something on the anniversary of Charles and Diana's wedding about a fresh wind. He has a many-faceted mind like his wife. Enjoyed watching the boys play 'touch' as I walked by shopping and mailing big-band tapes. You brought many people together when our walks are different. Here is a picture of Susie and Tim's daisy and clover wedding. Love, Byrd."

On our final Sunday at Barney Baptist the women of the church presented me with a friendship quilt. They each had created a square and put a Bible verse on it. Richie Langley, on behalf of the Sunday school, presented our boys with a big canvas bag from which they pulled dozens of baseball mitts, bats, balls, bases, a home plate, catcher's gear, and twelve blue hats and crisp white T-shirts that read Barney Baptist Bombers. "Now you can start a team," he said. He turned to Bob. "We are all thankful to you for always being there without fail, for having patience, and for lifting us up. Thank you, Pastor. Thank you, Wendy."

That last Sunday Bob and I and the boys stood in front of the congregation while the deacons prayed for us. I looked out at all the familiar faces, each one with a story. Jenny Little's eyes, though tear-filled, sparkled the way they always did. I thought of the battles we had waged on behalf of the missionaries, now a faded memory. She had been a sustaining force to Bob and me through hard times, writing us notes and assuring us of her prayers: "'When my heart is overwhelmed; lead me to the rock that is higher than I.' The Lord spoke to me through this verse when I spent some sleepless hours in prayer for you last night. God honors the faithful ministry of his special servants. I will pray for you and your new church. Our loss is their gain," she wrote in her farewell card.

I saw the faces of the SRC. Santa hadn't been back since that early battle, and we had found a way to bring back the Christmas tree. I don't know what became of the plastic Mary and Joseph.

Richie Langley, our helpful deacon, sat near Will and Lucy. I wondered what thoughts they all must have entertained about the rousing, tumultuous interlude the Zobas inhabited the parsonage. They were all longtime Barney residents and had weathered far more than the disruptions our brief tenure brought. Will had been nothing but smiles since the softball championship. His wife, Lucy, made us a farewell cheesecake.

Julie Munson sat in the front row with her unruly boys. They were climbing over and under the pews. She was disconsolate that Bob would no longer be stopping by to relieve her of her kids.

Donny Bodine made it out for that last Sunday. I looked up at him, and he gave me a thumbs-up. Addie Byrd sat perched like a chipmunk, her arms crossed in front of her resting on her knees. Ben Witherington stood at the back, holding bulletins, and I saw him pass one to Ernie Purdle, who showed up too. He sat with Gram, who was dotting her eyes with a tissue every time I looked at her. Deeter sat a few rows behind them. Seeing them made me think of Pop and crooked rows of green beans, giant cucumbers, and eating worms. He showed us all how to move past the damage we inflict on one another and how to start taking Communion again. In time, I took the little cup with the deep red juice again, and when I did, I thought about the literal blood of Jesus and how much blood it would take to fill the Communion cups of every Baptist church on every corner of every small town every first Sunday of every month.

I have come to understand (as much as one can understand) that the church is a mystery. We are the odd blend of human idiosyncrasies and holiness. Sometimes, when you're up to your ears in struggles, it's easy to miss that.

This is not to say that I don't still ask myself, *What is my place in this network of relationships? Who am I?*

In any case, I know who *they* are. They are the bride of Christ, and my husband is the groomsman. I am the one who takes the calls.

I can't say I understand why Jesus calls the church his bride. I can't say I understand why he entrusted to us the bride on the corner of Fourth and Birch. I can say this. When people ask me about God's mysterious ways, I think about Pop and the way he turned over the garden, good earth or dry as dust, one shovelful at a time. Sometimes the hardest thing to do is to put in a garden when the ground is hard. "You gotta keep turnin' it over. The harvest will come. You gotta believe that," he said. Even when you don't believe it, the actions make it so. I came to see that the church is like that, and so is the human heart. The Lord is the gardener, and we are the dry, hard earth that he keeps turning over and over until the soil is ready for the harvest to come. And it does.

We left our American flag in the parsonage, rolled up in the front closet. My husband's successor would surely be greeted by Mr. Patterson on the next national holiday. My geranium baskets were exploding that summer, wouldn't you know? I pulled up the garden I had put in by myself and took what remained of the harvest to Gram, in memory of Pop. The ground was hard when we started the digging, but we kept turning it over. Then the harvest came, just as Pop said.

PART THREE

BELIEVING LESSONS

9 *The Road Less Traveled*

To paster bob from francis. we will miss you your boys and dog. your are the best paster I ever had and the best one I will ever have in my life.

My husband was inundated with notes like this in June 1994 when we left the church he had served for four years in Tegucigalpa, Honduras. Our oldest son was to enter high school the following fall, and we wanted our boys to be in the United States for those years. It was time to move back.

For the season we served overseas, the people in our church were our "family." Many of them made careers out of an itinerant existence. They could end up anywhere. There were no assurances we would see some of them again. Saying "See you in heaven!" helped only a little.

The pain of those good-byes was intense, and it was compounded by the fact that our own future was uncertain. When the American Airlines 757 lifted us up and over the green mountains of that rugged landscape that June, we were bound for Cleveland; that much we knew. My husband's parents would meet us and deliver our sole possession: a Dodge Caravan they purchased for us with money we had left in a Stateside account. We had no forwarding address, no income, no idea where we would lay our heads over the course of the next several months.

That summer we meandered, three rowdy boys and a hundred-pound Labrador retriever named Bilbo, sharing space in the backseat of our Dodge Caravan. All of our worldly possessions were squeezed into the cartop carrier. From Ohio to North Carolina to Mississippi to Florida and back again, loving friends and gracious family took us in, dog and all.

If we had kept a travel log, it would have looked something like this:

Leaving Ohio for Asheville, early July: *"You mean to tell me you're going to drive all the way to Asheville in that car with those boys and that dog?"*

Asheville, where my sister kept the dog while we vacationed elsewhere for a week: *"What do you mean he pooped on the rug? Twice?"* (*"He misses you,"* she said.)

Leaving Asheville for Mississippi, late July: *"You sure you can make it all the way to Starkville in one day? With all the kids back there? And the dog?"*

Leaving Starkville for Asheville, early August: *"Does some-body keep hearing Willie Nelson singing in this car?"* (*"On the Road*

Again") *"We've got to get some Windex for these windows. Bilbo keeps slobbering."* *"How long are we going to be in Asheville this time, Mom?"* *"Where are we going next?"*

Leaving Asheville for Florida, mid-August: *"Are you really going to try to do this all in one day?"*

In Florida, Lupito's Restaurant, mid-September: *Bob and I celebrate our sixteenth wedding anniversary jobless and homeless.*

Leaving Florida for Asheville, late September: *"Haven't we done this before?"*

Leaving Asheville for Ohio, October 1.

That four-month sojourn, we were to discover, was the easy part of this journey.

We settled, sort of, in Bob's hometown in Ohio. His home church needed an interim pastor; we needed something to do. They had a house; we needed a home. So, that fall we lived in the church's parsonage, a block away from Bob's parents, while my husband started the process of getting re-networked. Bob initiated the necessary paper shuffling to reinvigorate his place in the pastoral job market while I put off my own networking in journalism until we had a clearer sense about where Bob might find a call.

Then the tide turned. It felt like a joke. Bob found himself entertaining serious prospects with four desirable churches. After months of wandering up and down the eastern United States, living out of suitcases and cleaning Bilbo's slobber off car windows, we found ourselves in the unlikely position of having a *choice*.

Of the four churches, we focused on a congregation in New Jersey. Having lived there once already, we had contacts and friends who were ready to pick up where we had left off four years earlier. And the church reminded us of the beloved congregation we had left behind in Honduras. It seemed a perfect fit. Bob arranged the candidating weekend. We figured we'd be moving into the four-bedroom parsonage before the new year.

I hadn't been looking for a job, nor had I entertained hope of pursuing my career goals at the expense of my husband's. So when I saw an ad in *Christianity Today* indicating that they were looking for an associate editor, it was almost tongue in cheek the way I said, "They have an opening that has my name on it."

They wanted a person who had journalistic experience and theological training, an odd and rare combination. I fit the bill. I had worked as feature writer and columnist for the English newspaper in Honduras and as the regional reporter for *Time* magazine. This, after majoring in religion during college (Greek and Hebrew did not help me negotiate grocery shopping in Honduras), and following up with a master's degree in theological studies. As a reporter in Honduras I probed hard issues like crimes against street children, child prostitution, and life in marginal communities. The thought of working for a magazine that highlighted church people and Holy Spirit topics seemed transporting.

My husband mused: "Send 'em a résumé."

The musing soon stopped.

Two weeks later, on a Tuesday, Bob and I sat stunned at our kitchen table. *Christianity Today* had offered me the job. They wanted my answer in a week. Their offices were located outside of Chicago. Bob, in the meantime, was scheduled to preach the following Sunday as the sole candidate for the pastoral position at the church in New Jersey. My husband had traveled with me to Chicago, where we met with editors and people who would be my colleagues. I traveled that weekend with him to New Jersey, where we met the flock who would be our new community and church family.

Every pew was filled that Sunday. My husband mounted the pulpit and preached the sermon of his life. They loved him. The sermon was a home run. I choked back the tears and started dismantling my dream.

Back in Ohio, Bob and I were nearly incapacitated. He couldn't bring himself to snuff out my dream of working for this magazine; I could not ask him to pass up this church. My yearnings lay to the west, where there were no assurances for anyone but me. No job for my husband. No home waiting for us to move into. No community to cook us supper until I got my kitchen set up. No preordained network of peers for our three sons. And my income alone would not sustain us. To the east, where my husband's dream lay, there awaited a four-bedroom parsonage with an above-ground pool and a two-car garage on a nicely lighted street in a neighborhood with manicured lawns. The church people were waiting.

Their youth pastor was excited to have three new male members in the youth group. The salary package more than covered our needs.

One is tempted to ask, What was the choice issue here?

Bob and I wandered through that week under a heavy silence. We didn't speak about it, sometimes for days. Each of us existed in the respective worlds dangled before us. I fantasized about issue layouts and meeting J. I. Packer. Bob worked through small-group strategies and started plotting out sermon topics for the coming year.

We were caught in the vortex of Ephesians 5: Paul tells wives to "submit to your husbands as you do to the Lord." He tells husbands, "Love your wives with the same love Christ showed the church [when] he gave up his life for her." How many weddings had my husband performed when brides squirmed and grooms smiled smugly at that first part and grooms started to sweat under the collar while brides got dewy-eyed at that second part?

This time *we* were squirming and sweating. Even meeting J. I. Packer could not justify what I would be asking of my husband and my family to pursue my side of this picture. About halfway through that hard week, Bob and I were lying on the bed, propped on elbows, sighing and moaning through an awkward silence. I surrendered. "I'll go call them and tell them I'm not coming."

He paused. "Don't call them yet," he said.

❊ ❊ ❊

Bob and I had met during our college years. In those days he wore his black curly hair in the white man's version of an Afro and sported an Amish beard, no mustache. He was the leader of the Christian fellowship group and had won a small but fiercely loyal following among the handful of Christians on campus. I was immediately impressed with his command of the Bible. He had an uncanny ability to make a meaningful and logical connection between it and real life without sounding dogmatic. And he stepped away from the circle when they started to sing "It Only Takes a Spark." I liked that.

At the beginning I did not feel attracted to him, which made for a friendly and animated "brother-sister" bond. We used the word *radical* a lot, along with *relevant* and (negatively) *mediocre*. We were "radical" Christians who were going to make biblical truths "relevant" for real life and refuse to settle for "mediocrity."

I was in my female-apostle-Paul phase then. He was hearing the call to celibacy. I was reading Dietrich Bonhoeffer's *The Cost of Discipleship* and memorizing 2 Corinthians 5—the whole chapter, not random verses. He was reading Fyodor Dostoyevsky and studying the Christian implications of South Africa's apartheid.

Unfettered by the strain of romantic confusion—he in his celibacy and I in my female-Paul radicalness—Bob felt free to lunch with me at the home of Mrs. Goodale, the elderly woman with whom I lived. We ate alfalfa-sprout sandwiches and sat on Mrs. Goodale's front porch swing talking about 2 Corinthians 5, apartheid, and how liberating it felt to answer the call to celibacy.

There was one small lapse in our respective callings, one

time, in Mrs. Goodale's living room. For a while after that, Bob avoided me. I lay in bed at night and closed my eyes and pictured myself lying on an altar, like a corpse on a funeral bier, and envisioned a stake going through my heart. I was sacrificing misguided inclinations.

I was not delivered. We were engaged within a few months and married before the year was out. So much for Paulness and celibacy.

Highfalutin as were those notions of radical discipleship, they did set the tone for our marriage. For better or for worse, *radical*—meaning "departing markedly from the usual; the extreme"—was the standard we had implicitly covenanted to uphold. We were to discover at any number of junctures in our common life that making the Bible "relevant" to real life demanded radicalness. We were also to discover that sometimes being radical can be crushing.

This was one of those moments. By the end of that week, as we pondered our prospective futures, our families had grown exasperated and our would-be employers, agitated. "Flip a coin!" our parents were telling us. The weight of our decision was bearing down.

It was around eleven in the morning at the end of that week when my husband approached me and put his arms around me. "I think we should take the road less traveled," he said. "I think we should move west, to Chicago."

I asked him why.

"Because it requires more faith."

The faith thing. It's radical. It can be heartbreaking. The book of Hebrews says faith is "the evidence of things we cannot yet see." That implies darkness. It implies groping through, wondering where you are, how you got here, and what is the way out. I was standing twenty feet away when Bob called the head of the pulpit committee at the New Jersey church. He explained, haltingly, why he could not accept the call. The man did not understand.

We were both scared and not a little confused.

Later that day, the same day Bob told me we should take the road less traveled, we received a letter that gave us some light. It came from a friend who had attended our church in Honduras. I will call her Laura. Laura was a visionary—you know the type—always hearing a "word from the Lord." Her letter was dated October 14, 1994. We received it six weeks later, in the last week of November.

> I am lying in bed—it's a long story—my back is killing me and now I can't even stand up or sit down, even lying is painful. Last week I told God I felt "cut down like a tree." He said I was not cut down but cut back that I might be "more fruitful."
>
> This morning I felt depressed again. Okay, Lord, I know you could have healed me by now if you wanted to. So what is it?
>
> [Her word from the Lord:] Write to Bob and Wendy.
>
> So, dear friends, I send you the letter I should have sent a long time ago. I don't ask how or what you are doing, for whatever it is, I know that you too have been "cut back" (pruned heavily) and are "sleeping in winter."

She's not all wrong there, I thought. I sat down with the letter.

> I hope you won't find this letter too strange. I could make it more "normal," but that would be allowing my mind to influence

an outcome that is not mine to influence. In truth, I am afraid of doing this. But because of my love for the Lord and my love for you, I must put fear aside.

Prophetic utterances are always a cause for fear and so-called prophets are always putting fear aside, I was thinking.

There is a nasty little shadow which skitters across my mind and says, What will they think? But the last time this thought was planted, my inner voice said, *Who are you that you should judge the rightness of the situation? Are you putting yourself before God?* Whoa! Strong words!

Prophetic utterances always involve inner voices.

For several days running I had many thoughts "of" and "for" you. (She was now referring to Bob and had addressed this portion of her "prophecy" to him.)

I don't remember it all, but I do remember the most important part—that God has something important for you to do, but it will take trust such as you have never been tested by, for it to come about.

Prophetic utterances always keep things in the vague future, like horoscope readings. Prophecy schmophecy!

Do you trust to the same degree as Abraham? Your trust will be stretched like a piece of elastic.

Nothing new there.

I see a road which diverges in two different ways.

I paused.

The right hand fork leads into a comfortable neighborhood.
The street is clean and wide and paved. There are
streetlights, so it is easy to see where to walk. But the light
is "man-made." The houses on this road are big four-bedroom
family homes.

I reread that sentence.

This road leads to a dead end. At the end is a large hall with the
words Hall of Plenty written over the archway of the front door.
People are happy there. There is laughter coming from this hall.
The people here are good people. They go to church. They
meet in brotherly fellowship. But they have not noticed that
God is not living there.

I started wondering what she would say about the *other* road.

The path to the left, well, it only just qualifies to be called a path.
I can hardly see it at all.

That doesn't sound good.

It is all in darkness, and the few feet of path I can see before it
twists out of sight are dirt tracks with potholes. You can know it
will not be easy to travel this pathway." (Here Laura includes a
marginal note: The going gets rough.)
    I see only one entrance, which is a tunnel into the thicket, made
naturally into an archway of twisted thorn and brambles. (Marginal
note: Stay in the center. If you bend slightly to left or right, you
get scratched/hurt.)
    The entrance is shoulder high, so you would have to stoop to
go in. (Marginal note: Need humility to enter.)
    Leaning against the entrance, against the brambles, is a shep-

herd's crook like Little Bo Peep's. Hanging on the "hook" of the crook is an unlit lantern.

Unlit? Why is the lantern unlit?

When your trust has been stretched like elastic, he will light the lantern. You must take the lantern and lead the way into the wood.

My palms were sweating.

"Fear not, for I am waiting on the other side. Listen to my voice, for I will keep calling to you so you will know which direction to head for. When you call my name, I will answer, and you will turn your face to me and keep walking towards me. If you forget to call upon my name, you will get lost in the darkness. Though the darkness be all about you, you will have my lantern and my staff by your side."

Blood rushed to my cheeks.

"I am being reminded of that poem by Robert Frost," Laura concluded.

> *Two roads diverged in a wood, and I—*
> *I took the road less traveled by,*
> *And that has made all the difference.*

Laura concluded her portion on Bob:

"Pity, your wood doesn't sound as inviting as Robert Frost's!!!"

❋ ❋ ❋

There have been moments when taking "the road less traveled" tendered very little light. We moved to the Chicago area, as planned, on faith. We held out hope that Bob would receive a pastoral call. Almost instantly he received an offer to serve as an interim at a small, struggling urban congregation in a first-ring Chicago suburb.

And, in keeping with the plan, I went to work on issue layouts and met J. I. Packer. The boys got settled in their respective schools. Bob sat with the Welcome Wagon lady and learned how to use the hot and cold settings on the washing machine.

Weeks stretched into months, into years. Bob did not receive a permanent call from the church of his dreams. That fleeting interlude back in Ohio, when we lingered over the profiles of four interested churches, was the last time we entertained the concept of choice. There were no "choices" for my husband on this road less traveled.

Thus began what Laura had called the season of trust, being "stretched like elastic." About a year and a half after we made this move, I took a day off from work to fast and pray. I wrote a prayer in my journal that day:

> It all started in Ohio, the day after Thanksgiving in 1994 when Bob gave up the call to go to New Jersey so that I could come and work here. You showed us miraculously, then, through Laura's letter, that this was the 'path' we were to take, thorny and dark though it may be. We have taken it. It has been both dark and thorny.
> How long, O Lord?
> Why have you given me the desires of my heart but at the expense of my husband's sense of purpose? He sacrificed himself. He 'gave himself up' for me, just as

you gave yourself up for the church. In three weeks it will be two years since he has carried a mantle. For two years he has struggled and questioned who he is.

I can barely keep from crying when I see others in satisfying work contexts where they have a sense of belonging and of wholeness. I see it all the time—people making comments about racquetball games and years of friendship with the same friends. All these good Christian people are blessed when my husband sacrificed his sense of purpose and doesn't have a friend in the world right now.

Lord, what do I say? We cannot earn your favor. You have said through your servant Peter, 'God is against the proud, but is always gracious to the humble.' Will you give grace now, Lord?

How do I pray? How long will he remain in the netherworld of not belonging? Will you give him friends who play racquetball and celebrate years of friendship? Will you give him a place of belonging? Lord, what do I pray?

✳ ✳ ✳

Our college days served us well. We kept hearing the voices of those radical thinkers we were reading back then, Bonhoeffer and Dostoyevsky. Once you've read Bonhoeffer's exposition of "cheap grace" and "costly grace," it is impossible to forget that grace "is costly because it costs a man his life, and it is grace because it gives a man the only true life." Once you've read Dostoyevsky's account of Alyosha Karamazov's conversion as he is weeping and falling down upon the earth, drenching it with his tears, it is impossible to forget the image of such love for life: "Every moment he felt clearly, almost physically, something real and indestructible, like the vault of the sky over his head, entering his soul. . . . He was a weak youth when he fell on the ground and he rose a strong and determined fighter."

"The way is unutterably hard and at every moment we are in danger of straying from it," Bonhoeffer wrote in *The Cost of Discipleship*. He was speaking of staying on "the narrow way" of the Christian walk. "If we are afraid of ourselves all the time, it is indeed an impossible way."

What did he mean, "if we are afraid of ourselves"? If we view our sojourn in this life from the human perspective? in human terms? Or, if we measure God's faithfulness according to how we feel or how it is going for us?

"If we behold Jesus Christ going on before, step by step, we shall not go astray," he wrote. "But if we worry about dangers that beset us, if we gaze at the road instead of Him who goes before, we are already straying from the path. For He is Himself the way, the narrow way and the straight gate. He, and He alone, is our journey's end."

Shortly before we were engaged, back in those nonmediocre, radical, and relevant days, we drew up what we called the "Bob-Wendy-Lord Covenant." In it we agreed to pray for each other, pray with each other, confess to each other, live in revealed truth, spend time "in the Word" alone, spend time in the Word together, "witness" together, sacrifice for each other, memorize Scripture, enter our "quiet times" expectantly and seeking, and share a truth from our quiet times with one another. We signed it April 16, 1978. We signed it again, in recommitment, November 2, 1980.

Things got complicated after that. We did the best we could.

Life's burdens and the passage of time have tempered us. But the fundamentals of our radical inclinations have remained in tact. My husband came to know the Lord through Dostoyevsky's book *The Brothers Karamazov*. The godly, searching lead character, Alyosha, inspired Bob during a dark season in his teen years when he questioned the reality of God in a world of such suffering and darkness. Father Zossima is the pious monk who mentors the young Alyosha. He teaches his protégé the way of love. "A true act of love, unlike imaginary love, is hard and forbidding. Imaginary love yearns for the immediate heroic act that is achieved quickly and seen by everyone," he says. "A true act of love, on the other hand, requires hard work and patience, and for some, it is a whole way of life." Alyosha convinced my husband that the Christian faith is authentic and real, even amid a world of suffering and evil. In a way, this kind of love is forbidding, absent of heroic flourishes. It is the kind of love that makes illogical choices and then suffers under those choices but still walks forward, even in the dark, waiting for the light.

It ended up that Bob became the full-time pastor at that small church he had served as an interim. The pulpit committee never held a single meeting the whole time he served as interim because they knew they wanted him as their pastor. It hasn't been easy because of the distance involved and the changing demographics of the neighborhood. But he is receiving cards and notes again, like the one little Francis sent him when we left our church in Honduras.

We have stopped measuring our lives in terms of dreams realized or lost. Maybe we were weak like Alyosha was as the youth who fell to the ground and soaked the earth with his tears. Maybe someday, like Alyosha, we will reach the place where we rise strong and more determined. In the meantime, we are living in the realm of "the realized will," to borrow a phrase from Jim Elliot: "To dream and want and pray almost savagely; then to commit and wait and see him quietly pile all dreams aside and replace them with what we could not dream." We have learned that sometimes God's most powerful movements are played out in his silence. I read in Oswald Chambers, "Faith in the Bible is faith in God against everything that contradicts Him—I will remain true to God's character whatever He may do. 'Though he slay me, yet will I trust Him'—the most sublime utterance of faith in the whole Bible."

Along the road less traveled you learn to pray as the psalmist did, "You are my portion, O Lord."

I should note that Laura's prophecy letter had an "utterance" for me: "Hey, Wendy! *Lighten up.* Heavenly joke. Pun intended. Don't worry. Let your light shine." In other words, there is blessedness even on dark roads with thickets of twisted thorn and brambles. I saw a picture of it one evening during the early phase of this traveled road. Our boys were younger and still in the home, and we were sharing family devotions. I don't remember the passage from the Bible we read, but I remember the discussion that followed.

My husband asked our boys, "Are you happy in the Lord?"

Our then-thirteen-year-old, Jon, answered, "Yes."

Bob asked, "Why are you happy?"

"Because I can do cross-country and it's fun," said Jon.

"Could you be happy if you weren't in cross-country?"

"Yes," Jon said, "because I have lots of friends."

"Could you be happy if you didn't have lots of friends?"

Jon didn't answer.

Maybe being "happy in the Lord" means a kind of happiness not rooted in having things. Maybe that kind of happiness is not found in getting everything we want when we want it. When Jesus sent out seventy-two disciples, they returned elated and abuzz with the thrill of their successes in ministry— healing this and that disease, casting out demons. Jesus said to them, "Don't rejoice just because evil spirits obey you; rejoice because your names are registered as citizens of heaven." It was as if Jesus were saying to them, "Could you be 'happy' serving me if the demons *hadn't* submitted to you?"

On the road less traveled it was as if the Lord were asking my husband, "Could you be happy doing my will if you *didn't* have your station in life right where you wanted it, if all your career goals haven't been met?"

We ended our devotions that night by getting on our knees and thanking God that our names were written in heaven. That his love for us doesn't change, even when our circumstances do, and that his love cannot be taken away from us. We finished praying. Bob fixed himself on the couch. "I'm happy in the Lord," he said.

10 *Visions*

For reasons I can't understand or explain, Murrays receive visions. Sometimes the visions are mundane and pragmatic: In 1959, when my mother was pregnant with her fourth child, my father, Myles Murray, received a vision that called him to leave his place of employment and start his own business in the family basement. (Scratch "pragmatic.") Sometimes the visions have been ethereal and otherworldly, downright weird. These kinds of visions were the forte of my grandmother, Sara Murray, whom we affectionately called Button.

Button was prone to seeing strange things in everyday moments. On more than one occasion when I was a girl she recounted to me remarkable visitations that she swore were direct revelations from the Lord, revelations that teased the bounds of even this young girl's fancy, and I used to sing to trees pretending they were my boyfriends. But I have come to understand that we can find something of God in these extraordinary visitations, and more to the point, sometimes these are the places he shows himself most clearly.

There was the time Button was standing on her back porch braiding her hair while my grandpa was locking the henhouse door. She looked over the field up to the sky and saw, clear as day, a huge cross that covered the deep blue evening sky "from north to south, as far as your eye could see, pure white like a white ribbon," she said. The corners of the cross were as sharp as the edges of paper.

Then my grandpa saw a black cloud come out of nowhere. "Look up there," he said. Button looked and saw the same black cloud hanging close to the ground. It split at the top, making a V, and began pouring itself out at the bottom in a stream of crimson red, "the color of blood."

"God is my judge, I'm telling the truth. On your grand-dad's deathbed he told your daddy to believe it 'cause he saw it. It is hard for the human mind to believe, but I dare not deny it," she said.

The way I saw it then—and still do—was, well, if my grandmother saw visions, then she earned them. She raised three sons during the depression, my father among them, with an alcoholic husband who burned down the farm. If she said the Lord came to her in a white cross stretched across a sapphire-blue evening sky with a blood-dripping cloud, who was I to say she didn't?

I was ten when Button told me about her vision of the white stone. I was sitting at her kitchen table, where years' worth of grime stuck to the red-checkered plastic tablecloth. Her kitchen was small and greasy and smelled like bacon and

lye. But it had windows, and the sunshine brightened it.
Sitting at Button's kitchen table made me think of hot milk
and the raisin-filled cookies she used to make, soft and
gooey inside. That day she was wearing a cotton dress, tied at
the back, with delicate purple and yellow flower bouquets on
it. It made her robust figure look like a poster from the
1940s. Her auburn hair had only traces of gray, and she tied
it up in a bun. I can still see her turning and looking at me
while she used a wooden spoon to stir scrambled eggs in the
cast-iron frying pan. She held that frying pan with one hand
like it wasn't heavier than a fly swatter. Before the vision
story, however, she smiled and asked me if I ever heard a
dog talk.

I looked up. "No."

Sam, a nondescript, long-haired, bronze-colored mutt,
was waiting at her feet for something to drop. "Sam can talk.
He says, 'I want meat,'" said Button. She turned the flame to
low and took a piece of bologna from the fridge. She held it
over Sam's nose. "Say, 'I want meat.'"

Sam didn't speak.

"Say, 'I want meat,' Sam. Come on, now."

Sam barked three times. It sounded like a ventriloquist
saying "I want meat"—*rye/rah/reeh*. Button chortled a laugh that
came straight from her belly and tossed Sam the bologna.

I wondered that she could laugh like that given the hard-
ship that colored her world, but Button showed me it was
possible to laugh and suffer at the same time. One aspect of
my grandmother's tortured and mystical life was raising
three boys, my father being the middle son. They lived in

Liverpool, Pennsylvania, population six hundred, and she did her best to raise them in church. My father remembered Button as having been "mostly impressed with the punishing God," which panicked him enough to go forward more than once, as a young boy, when the parson issued the weekly altar call. But Button possessed a softer side, which my father also knew. Each year for his birthday she made him his favorite devil's food cake with sour milk, and at Christmas she made raisin-filled cookies and hung up her sons' black socks, filled with hard candy and an orange in the toe. On New Year's she cooked fried oysters and pork sauerkraut.

My father left his hometown by way of the U.S. Army. "It was good-bye Liverpool, poverty, family strife, and stagnation," he wrote in a memoir. He made it to college, met my mother, started that business in the family basement, and walked away from the faith of his youth, such as it was. This had always been a source of heartache for my grandmother.

"I was thirty-three, and my life was full of heartaches and poverty," she said, getting back to the story about the vision of the white stone. "I was heavyhearted and couldn't pray." Her husband, my grandpa, had died shortly after I was born, so I never knew him. But the vision took place when he was still living.

"Your grandfather was a decent man, but he drank," she continued. "Your daddy and his brothers were a pack of trouble back then. I went into my bedroom when I was having one bad day and sat on the floor. I wasn't kneeling like you do for prayer. I sat there with my legs out in front of me and my head leaning on the side of the bed. I cried for a while. Then I looked up, and in front of me I saw a hand holding a white stone between the thumb and the first finger. The fingers were white, and the stone was off-white. I prayed, 'Dear God, don't let me lose my mind.'"

Button turned off the fire on the stove and slid into the chair next to mine at the kitchen table. She put her elbows on the table and rested her chin in her hands. "About a month later I told my Uncle John—a saint if God ever made one—because I knew he wouldn't laugh at me, and he didn't. He told me to go get my Bible and open it to Revelation chapter 2, verse 17."

Button asked me to get her King James Bible off the coffee table. Then she opened it and read that verse: "He that hath an ear, let him hear what the Spirit saith unto the churches; To him that overcometh will I give to eat of the hidden manna, and will give him a white stone, and in the stone a new name written, which no man knoweth saving he that receiveth it."

The sun was slicing through the kitchen window, and Sam lay pacified at my grandmother's feet. My elbows stuck to the plastic tablecloth. Button looked at me through a sheen of wetness in her eyes. "God promised me a new name." She smiled faintly and rose to stir the eggs.

That was my first exposure to the possibility of visions. I never doubted Button's story. When the issue came up again many years later—years after Button had died—I was inclined toward belief rather than doubt.

✳ ✳ ✳

We discovered in 1993 my father had prostate cancer. We thought it had been eradicated when he underwent surgery shortly thereafter. In fact, my family and I were far more concerned about his other health problems, his emphysema and heart fibrillation. My father heroically battled through each day as these ailments conspired to make him suffer. It took my sisters, my brother, my mother, and me by surprise when it became clear that the cancer, not the spasmodic heart or damaged lungs, would be the death of him. He began his rapid decline in August 1995. That's when he posted his last e-mail message. It was to my husband:

> *Date: Aug 15, 1995*
> *Subj.: The Power of Prayer*
>
> Dear Bob: your prayers must have done it. Last nite i couldnt get in or out of bed without help. at 5 i woke up in wet sheets that were soaked from sweat. my pain was relieved almost entirely. it wont stay away but this is ok. thank you for your prayers. love dad.

We did pray, all the time, for my dad. Although we didn't know how to pray or what to pray for, we rejoiced with him that day when his pain melted away into a bundle of wet sheets. But I knew, as my father did, that all the prayers in heaven and on earth would not deliver him—and us—from this course. We knew his pain would come back.

And it did. In the course of the last weeks of my father's

life, we waited and watched as he slowly left us. Apart from the bright yellow Do Not Resuscitate orders pasted indecorously on his bedroom wall, my father surrendered his dying into the hands of God, and we did too.

We watched helplessly as he stopped coming out to the kitchen table for meals. Then he stopped sitting up in his bed for meals. Then he stopped eating altogether. Then he stopped drinking. We saw him move from emotional connection to this life into quiescent assurance of his eternal destination. This eventually gave way to paranoiac agitation, to delirium, to incoherence, and finally, to silence.

He suffered. And we suffered, too. But neither he, nor we, took back the choice to let God have his way in this death, even when the pain and sense of powerlessness were so acute that we pondered the strangeness of God's way of doing things. God met us there. We could not have imagined or scripted how he carried us through. And we would not have been able to see it or receive it if we had not been in a place where we felt the darkness overtaking us.

At the time, my parents were living in Florida and I in the Chicago area. The distance between us accentuated my feeling of helplessness during these final stages. At certain points the best I could do was to pray for him. I wrote in my journal dated August 22, 1995: "What could I give him now? It is only you he needs. Only you can meet him where he is. I know you are there because, all along, you have always met us where we were. There are no words I could say or gestures I could make to take his pain away. That he would see you, even in the midst of his pain, that he could behold your beauty in these moments, that is my prayer for him now. Touch him, dear Lord, that his countenance would testify to your presence."

God answered that prayer. The answer came during one of my father's more alarming episodes in the undignified dying process. His body was weakening, and functions that were once automatic had become heroic. He was reduced to painfully humiliating exercises. That's when God came to him and gave him his vision.

For a long time as he declined, my father had maintained his bodily functions on his own. This was not easy, even before the cancer weakened him. He was encumbered by laboring lungs and the awkwardness of lugging around his oxygen tank.

One night, in late August, he awoke around four in the morning needing a trip to the bathroom. My mother had insisted he should waken her during such moments. That night my dad felt sure he could make it on his own, so he found his way to the bathroom. On the way, however, he discovered that the cannula, the tubing for his oxygen supply, would not reach the distance. He removed it for the few minutes it would take, laying the tubing down on the floor, and proceeded to the bathroom. When he came back out, he could not find the cannula.

This was his moment: A onetime inventor, artist, collector, philanthropist, and CEO of that successful company he started in the family basement—now a grown, sick man—was crawling around on the floor, mustering strength his decrepit, dying body did not have, groping for his oxygen tubing.

He called for my mother.

Then he looked up. He was someplace else. He was on a train. It came out of a tunnel and arrived on a different track. The man said, "Don't worry; you have a new job." He told my dad to pick out his new clothes. My dad picked "the grubbies, not robes," he told us later.

My mother reached him and replaced the cannula into his nostrils. Life-giving oxygen brought him back. With my mother's help, he made his way back into the bed.

The next morning he was a different person. The only thing my father could speak about was what he had seen and felt when that train came out of the tunnel onto the different track, landing him in the new and wonderful place where he picked out his new clothes.

My sister Carol was in Florida with my parents when this episode occurred. The following day my father asked her to write down his remembrances of this vision: "I had a total physical, mental, and spiritual journey. Spiritually, I am whole. I feel as if I have been transfigured into an intellectual property of God.

"I don't know how long I can stay [in this life]. This is okay. In fact, I'm happy, elated. I know the promises of Jesus are true. I know they are not empty promises. It is the most wonderful feeling. I'm safe from further embarrassment.

"I am on a new clock. I am glad to know that. I will be starting my new time from August 29, 1995, at 4:25 A.M. That's my new date. What I have been through is a signal. I wouldn't have said anything if it were not true.

"The promises of Jesus are worth it. They are not shallow

promises. I've picked out my new clothes. I picked out grubbies, not robes. There are a lot of people there like me. People's prayers have been successful. There is not a continuing need to pray anymore, no more praying to keep me here. Spiritually, I am complete, though the body is weak. I will see Kelly and buddy up with her right away.

"I am not a nut," he concluded. "Everything that happened seemed to me to really happen." All "the fuss" with hospice care and the meds "really didn't matter," he said.

I visited my father shortly after this episode. Before I arrived at their house I felt some apprehension. I was afraid to see my father dying. I remember as a little girl of about eight, lying in my bed, unable to sleep, tormented by the fear of my parents dying. I rose and went downstairs crying and afraid. I found my father sitting on the couch in the living room and told him of my fears. He sent me back to my room and told me to think about why pine trees are pointed at the top. I figured it out in about ten minutes and went back downstairs, unpacified. This time he came up to my room and lay with me on my bed. Comforted by his presence, I finally drifted off to sleep. That day, going into this visit, I felt like that same little girl. Only this time my deepest fears were playing out.

Walking into his bedroom, where my mother and some friends were sitting with him, I knew instantly this was the only place for me to be. I hugged him, and he told me I looked pretty. He held my hand. It surprised me. (He hadn't been the hand-holding type.) He told me he wasn't in actual pain at the moment, just "distress—I can't get comfortable—

but no pain." I left after half an hour to let him rest. Only a few minutes passed before he pressed his buzzer and asked me to come back into his room. He wanted to pray for me. He was sitting up in bed. I sat next to him, and he put his arm around me. I put my arm around him. He prayed quite vigorously. He thanked the Lord for all his children, "especially my Wendy," he said. (I'm sure he said that to all the sisters when he prayed with them, but it meant a lot.) He prayed for my husband and sons, that they would get over the sicknesses they were combating. I quickly realized there were not enough tissue boxes in that bedroom. I had to hunt some down after he finished praying for me.

During these visits I would read to my father from the *Daily Light* devotional booklet for morning and evening devotions. My mother would sit next to him on the bed and hold his hand while I read. An especially meaningful devotion included these portions of Scripture: "I shall be satisfied, when I awake, with thy likeness." "The night is far spent, the day is at hand." "He shall be as the light of the morning, when the sun riseth, even a morning without clouds; as the tender grass springing out of the earth by clear shining after rain." Reading those made me realize that my father's countenance after his "heavenly journey" (as we called it) was like that: like a cloudless morning with tender grass shining and springing out of the earth after a rain.

He had changed. He was more intensely himself than I have ever known him. His face was pale and sunken, unshaved and dry, but at the same time there was a sublimity and serenity about him that I had never seen before.

He was grateful for every little thing I did. And, really, I did so little. I covered his feet, rubbed his back, refreshed his dry mouth with lemon-glycerin swabs, and it felt like a sacrament. There was so much more I wish I could have done.

※ ※ ※

My father's pain management soon moved to a new level, which sadly interrupted the joyful interlude in the aftermath of his vision. He could no longer tolerate the pain with Vicodin only. The time had come to introduce M S Contin— morphine. By the end of the first week of the new drug, my father's behavior was dramatically altered. He woke up in the middle of the night another time, panic-stricken that he did not have enough oxygen. He wanted to call 9-1-1. We as a family had all agreed *not* to do that under any circumstances. (We were prepared to call hospice in the event of an emergency.) We feared they would be compelled to begin heroic measures to preserve his life, perhaps putting him on a respirator, which contradicted his own desires. My bed-ridden, frail father, who under normal circumstances at this stage could not brush his own teeth, wrestled my mother for the phone and dialed 9-1-1 himself.

Despite our apprehensions, my mother sang praises when the paramedics arrived. They sedated my father. They did not put him on a respirator, and we were thankful.

"The diagnosis is clear," my brother-in-law, who is a doctor, wrote to the family over the Internet the next day. "Delirium."

The disorientation and hallucinations, the "waxing and

waning sensorium," were the classic hallmarks of delirium, he
said. Adjusting medication and "maintaining oxygenation"
will help, but some degree of delirium would probably
continue. "There will be times of relative lucidity, though
these times will be fewer and farther between as time goes on."

I stared out the window of the 737 as its wings and thrusters,
by now my familiar friends and partners in mission, lifted
me another time, up and away, on what I was sure would be
my final assignment in this ordeal: to pack my father off to
heaven.

When I arrived that evening, he was asleep on his side. He
had settled down, and the delusions had subsided, for a time
anyway. He lay on one side of the king-sized bed; the other
side was reserved for family visits, fully equipped with an
extra blanket, a study pillow, and plenty of tissues. I crawled
up on the other side. The only light in the room came from
the white Christmas lights on the Norfolk Island pine my
sister had sent him. We had decorated it with handmade
picture ornaments of all of his grandchildren smiling back at
him. The quiet hum of the concentrator, the source of his
oxygen supply, had a calming effect and filled the room,
almost, with a sense of peaceful control. He knew I was
there. He had no strength but managed to lift his arm so I
could take his hand. His limbs were cold. I told him not to
stay awake for me, to go ahead and sleep. I prayed out loud
anyway. I wanted him to hear how grateful to God I was for
his life. His breathing was sporadic. He twitched a lot.

My brother-in-law was right. The delirium continued up

to the last days of my father's consciousness. He had paranoiac frenzies about not having enough oxygen even though
his concentrator was set at its highest setting within the
bounds of safety. We found him once pulling on his cannula
the way he used to pull our boat into the dock during summer weekends at the lake. "I'm docking the boat," he said.
He wanted his wristwatch all the time even though he didn't
know what day it was. He asked me one time how I could live
with so much junk in my house. (This may have been a
coherent moment.) When the minister came into the room
once, my father thought he was my mother.

This stage was particularly painful for me. I felt, strangely,
that I was more a source of frustration for Dad than a comfort. I didn't know the ins and outs of his oxygen management, so I couldn't authoritatively assuage his paranoiac
ravings. I said things like, "The lights are on" and "Everything
is connected." I wasn't strong enough to lift him and help him
get positioned comfortably, and when I tried once, the sheet
got caught so that I was lifting him up while the sheet was pulling him down. (He cursed that time.) I knew he needed us.
The hospice chart had us down as "very supportive family."
But there were passages of this ordeal that made me feel as if
my whole life I did everything all wrong.

My brother-in-law was also correct when he said there
would be lucid moments. My three sons joined me later on
this final visit. When they arrived, the boys came to the
bedside to greet him.

Ben went in first, kissed him, and said, "I love you,
Grandpa."

My dad said, "I love you, too." But he mistakenly called Ben "Jon." Ben went along.

Then Jon hugged him and kissed him and said, "I love you, Grandpa."

Dad said, "Oh, *you're* Jon. Sorry, Ben! I love you too, Jon."

Our oldest son, Nate, kissed him. Dad said, "Now how long before you go back to Chicago?"

"Not for several more days."

"Well, then we have plenty of time," he said.

He sensed a houseful of family, and it comforted him. Later that weekend he said he wanted a "family dinner," the way we used to have them on Sundays. He'd cook and carve the beef Wellington, and Mom would make hot German potato salad. This time it was tapioca pudding. My boys, my brother, his wife, my mother, and I took our little plastic cups of pudding and gathered around his bed for "family fellowship."

He vacillated between moments like these and those scary spells when he wasn't himself. But it was not long before both tendencies lapsed into incoherence and almost total unconsciousness. We checked him regularly, about every half hour, to make sure his cannula was connected and that he was covered. To see if he was still breathing.

Once when I checked him, I found him awake. I sat on the bed with him. "Is everything all right?" I asked.

He took my hand and squeezed it. He had strength. "Everything's fine," he said. "I love you, honey."

"I love you, too." I rubbed his cold arm until he went back to sleep.

My plans to see him off to heaven fell through. He didn't die before I had to get back on the plane. I despaired over leaving him. I knew he was close to the end. But, as we had done from the beginning of this passage, I had to relinquish control.

He died two days later. My mother was with him. My sister had been sleeping in the living room outside his bedroom. She was strangely awakened in time to see my mother holding his hand, and then, to hear his last breath. She went to wake up my brother in the next room and my brother-in-law, the doctor, who pronounced him dead—to the family, anyway.

❄ ❄ ❄

Later in Button's life, when I was grown and had children of my own, she and I wrote letters. "I am old and weary. I just never seem to see any change in the life of some of those I love so dearly," she wrote one time. She was referring to her three sons, all of whom drank at some point in their lives, as their father had. My dad quit drinking in 1972, and Button saw that miracle. But he hadn't yet returned to the faith she had instilled when he was a boy, which remained a source of deep sorrow for Button. I sent her a picture of my oldest son as a baby, sitting on my father's lap. "I was so glad to get the picture you sent," the letter continued. "Your dad looked so real I felt I had to touch him. And your baby is so sweet and has such beautiful eyes. I could see in your dad's face a happiness no one else but that baby could put there. God will answer. A miracle will happen, you'll see. Let's pray for a miracle."

Button did not live to see that miracle. She died in 1988, just as my father was starting to find his way back to the faith of his youth. She never heard him say, "All the promises of Jesus are true. There are no empty promises."

Maybe that's why God gave Button visions. It seems they came in dark moments, when she needed a glimpse of something else, something more real than her circumstances. Sometimes her visions were so real, so close to God, they seemed unreal. Button feared no one would believe her when she tried to explain them. My father kept repeating, "I am not a nut" when he told us about his.

The prophet Ezekiel said the same thing: "O Sovereign Lord, they are saying of me, 'He only talks in riddles!'" There seemed no end to the pain God expressed through this tormented prophet. The book abounds with lament after lament, bizarre visitations, and emotive proclamations of judgment and pain. And there were visions. "Son of man, look toward Jerusalem." "Son of man, groan before the people!" "Son of man, give the people [a] message." "Son of man, cry out and wail; pound your thighs." "Son of man, prophesy to them and clap your hands vigorously. Then take the sword and brandish it twice, even three times." "Son of man, make a map and trace two routes . . . for . . . Babylon." Those were the instructions he received in chapter 21 alone. The visions, one would presume, helped get him through the torment. "The Lord took hold of me, and I was carried away by the Spirit of the Lord. . . . He asked me, 'Son of man, can these bones become living people again? . . . Speak to these bones. . . . Speak to the winds.'"

❊ ❊ ❊

The death of a loved one brings into odd juxtaposition the grief of living in the hard places of this world and the hope of the realness of that other world, the one we see only in glimpses, the one just beyond our reach. That second world becomes more real during such interludes.

I wasn't sad the day of my father's memorial service. It was a good day. We celebrated him that day. We laughed and remembered funny moments, like the time he bought a golf cart and drove it for the first time down his driveway and took out two mailboxes in the process. Still, we are left to wonder why death must be preceded by so many twists and turns before it has its way with us.

In the aftermath of Dad's death, I paused when I saw his wheelchair folded up and stored in the garage. How many times had I pressed my hand between the arms to open it quickly so Dad could be wheeled to the bathroom? I remembered his feet shuffling along to keep up. I saw the sipper mug I would put to his mouth so he could take water. How many times had I filled that mug with fresh bottled water and a squirt of lemon? I paused when I saw my mother doing the laundry. She tossed into the basket the T-shirts we had cut up the back to get on and off him, and the boxers he was wearing the last time I saw him.

Surrendering a loved one's death into God's hands certainly takes us to places we don't want to go. But God comes to us in those places. In fact, he resides in those places, and if we are looking for it, he gives us visions to see a clearer picture. The darkness of those hard places gives us the eyes to see. He surprises us. It is in the dark places we see him for who he is.

Before my father died, I had prayed to God in helplessness, "It is only you he needs. That he would see you and behold your beauty in these dark moments." My father was right when he wrote to my husband in that last e-mail, "There is power in prayer." My father's assurance spoke prophetically about what would be required of all of us to get through this passage.

To this day I honestly couldn't say why pine trees are pointed at the top. Whatever I came up with that night when I was a tormented little girl in my bed so many years ago, it was enough for my father to reckon he'd better find another way to settle my fears.

David Brainerd, the Puritan missionary to the Indians, died at age twenty-nine. He wrote in his diary, "I could with great composure look death in the face, frequently with sensible joy." When the time came for my sisters, my brother, my mother, and me to pack Dad off to heaven, I was not that terrified little girl. I looked at his death with a sensible joy. I was comforted by the change I saw after his "heavenly journey." It was a trade-off. His presence comforted me as a child while my fears bound me up. When he died, my fears were released, but so was his presence.

When I think of my Grandmother Button, I see white crosses floating in the evening sky and black clouds converging in a V dripping crimson blood. I see a white stone held between a thumb and an index finger that promised Button a new name. When I think of my father, I think about the "grubbies" and about pine trees. Button got her new name; my father got his new clothes—emphasis in both cases on *new*. Their visions pointed upward, like pine trees, to someplace else. To a place most of us neither see nor understand. They had to make the case for it. They felt as if they had to defend their sanity, like Ezekiel, who complained, "They are saying of me, 'He only talks in riddles!'"

Unbelievably, not too long ago I saw a special segment on the news that asked the question: "Have you ever wondered why pine trees are pointy at the top?"

Yes, I heard myself say. *I have wondered that.*

"They are competing for survival to see which one will be the king of the trees," the report noted perceptively. You can lop off the point, and it will raise up a new bud, just like that, the report said. "They are fiercely determined to be pointy. It's a shape that has worked for millions of years."

Now why didn't I think of that?

Before my father died, but after his heavenly vision, I asked him, "Could you see earth while you were in heaven?"

"Oh yeah," he said. "There's not much distance between them. Really, they're supposed to be all one."

I believe him.

Sometimes I have wondered how I can live the rest of my days without hearing my dad's voice on the other end of the phone. That's when I think about pine trees. That's how I finally figured out why they are pointed. They are fiercely determined to point upward, to show us the way to heaven, where the real world is.

11 Jesus Freaks

You've buried your father. You've moved your mother into a retirement community. You've packed two of your three children off to college. You're looking at your last year with your final child at home. You're thinking about opportunities missed, and regrets, and dreams that aren't going to come true on this side of eternity. You're not sleeping well—the scourge of hormones and hot flashes. You look in the mirror and aren't sure who you're looking at. You're asking yourself, Is God in this picture? You lift your face to heaven, but you can't see him.

When I became a Christian in the early 1970s, I fancied myself the ultimate Jesus Freak. I parted my hair in the middle, didn't wear a bra, and sang "He Ain't Heavy, He's My Brother" in the name of Jesus. I was a hippie Christian who found that lovin' feeling, full of warmth and intimacy, through Christ. I remember the picture in *Life* magazine back then that captured the essence of the Jesus movement.

And indeed it was a picture of my own faith as a teen convert. A young woman in cutoffs and a denim shirt with the word *Jesus* painted on the back was standing in shallow water—it was a baptismal scene—with her head tilted back, eyes closed, her arms splayed and raised, palms up, as if receiving fullness and blessing from above. The Jesus people, my people, were disciples in cutoffs, ecstatic, worshipful, high on Jesus with arms wide open grabbing the loving embrace of the living God. That photograph in *Life* of the Jesus Freak "receiving" captures the essence of the spirituality I owned as a teen, as if God existed *for me,* rather than the other way around.

But when you face a passage of life where your reality is defined more by losing than by receiving, such a view of the Christian walk becomes untenable. You start to feel as if, in addition to everything else, you are also losing God.

In the meantime, two of my sons, Ben and Jon (ages nineteen and seventeen at this writing), have owned the Christian faith and have captured a vision of God I did not perceive in my Jesus Freak days. To my surprise, they have enlarged my perception of God, and so, in turn, have helped steady me amid a turbulent passage.

The differences in our outlooks at conversion struck me most markedly when recently I came upon the little brown journal I kept as a new convert. Thirty years later I have had occasion to observe my sons' spiritual reflections, and the disparity is noteworthy:

Me (as a new teen convert): "Sometimes I feel so warm inside. Jesus is that warmth."

Them (as teen converts): "Who are we compared to this God? We are nothing; we are but filthy rags that need to be sent to the fire pit. We are weeds. We are undesirables."

Me: "I feel fine. Jesus is with me. Sharing my feelings about the Lord with other people makes it easier to feel him and understand him."

Them: "God cannot look at us because we are dirty. We spit in God's face, the one who created us and the universe. Why do we still live after we spit in the most holy God's face? Because he loves us. His love is not human love. In fact, his love is so great that we cannot fully understand it."

Me: "Sometimes it's so hard to love. But love is such a beautiful trip."

Them: "I felt the glory and awesomeness of God. I fell on my face and wept because of how awesome he is. Then I wept because I reject him by sinning. Then I wept because he forgives even me."

Me: "Jesus is more than someone to look up to in the sky and pray to. He's a friend. He's with you always. I love Jesus so much. Sometimes I feel so close to the Lord I want to reach out and touch him. It's such a beautiful feeling."

Them: "How hopeless! There is no reason to live! There is no reason for somebody to live unless he is a Christian. God created everyone. He made us to bring glory to God, for no other reason. *No* other reason."

Me: "Faith in Jesus can ease your mind of life's problems. Love in Jesus can make the world beautiful. Hope can give your life meaning. Faith, love, hope—what a combination."

Them: "He uses some pots for noble purposes, and he

makes some to destroy. God does the same thing with humans. Yes, he makes some humans to die. What right does God have to kill us? Maybe the question should be, What right do we have to live?"

Me: "Smile. Jesus is alive. He lives with us, for us. Don't be sad. Why be sad? Jesus is here, and he loves us. So smile!"

Them: "How great this God is who can kill us! This God who can split the Red Sea. God is the only one who can send us to hell. God can reject us if he wants to. After all, he is God."

Ben first owned the faith as a young child of four. My husband and I would talk to him about giving his life to Jesus. While Ben had always exhibited the heart of God, extending selfless and kind gestures (disciplines it takes a lifetime of sanctification to acquire), it troubled and perplexed us when he stubbornly resisted our invitations for him to give his life to Christ. He offered no explanations. He simply said in his preschool English that he wasn't ready.

After months of resistance, one morning as we sat at the kitchen table eating Cheerios, little Ben announced he was ready to give his life to Jesus. He got up from the table and went upstairs. My husband and I looked at each other and then followed him. We expected to find Ben by his bed on his knees in prayer. We didn't. We found him folding his Star Wars pajamas into his Sesame Street suitcase.

"Ben, what are you doing?"

"Packing."

"Why?"

"To go to heaven," he said.

Then we understood why our child had hesitated so stubbornly for so long. He thought giving his life to Jesus meant leaving us and taking up residence, literally, with him in heaven.

Our son Jon came to his understanding of the faith in a strikingly different way. In the summer of 1999 he and Ben had been on a wilderness trip to Colorado with their youth group. After their return, Jon shared his testimony at church about how the trip had changed his life because he captured a new and powerful vision of God. "On the bus ride at night there was an amazing storm, not like the thunderstorms here in Illinois. It was, like, nonstop lightning. I was so humbled in the sight of the Lord. God opened my eyes and let me see his greatness. I saw his omnipotence. It made me realize how frail humans are and how insignificant we are in comparison with God's power. He is awesome. It made me tremble at the thought. I heard God speak to me during that storm."

Well, we in the pews were wondering, *what did he say?*

"It was like he said—'I could smash you like an ant.'"

I should note that my sons are five-point Calvinists. The five "points" spell the word *TULIP,* an acrostic derived from the following theological essentials: **T**otal depravity, **U**nconditional election, **L**imited atonement, **I**rresistible grace, and **P**erseverance of the saints. Ben and Jon have each come to own this understanding of the faith separately and to defend it fiercely.

A significant influence on their understanding of the Christian faith has been the preaching and writings of John Piper, pastor of Bethlehem Baptist Church in Minneapolis, Minnesota, or, as Ben calls him, "the biggest stud ever." My sons went to hear him preach when he was in town about a year ago. He preached—or I should say, "laid the smack down"—about "faith that rescues and faith that endures," from Hebrews 11, including the following verses: "Some faced jeers and flogging, while still others were chained and put in prison. They were stoned; they were sawed in two; they were put to death by the sword. They went about in sheepskins and goatskins, destitute, persecuted and mistreated—the world was not worthy of them."

Ben told me about it later on: "Fifteen of us [guys from their youth group, Piper groupies all] were sitting in the front pew. I can still hear him [in Piperesque intonations]: 'We must always remember whether you are saved by your faith and are enabled to endure suffering by your faith; whether we suffer or are rescued by our suffering; the determining factor is not the amount of your faith. No. The determining factor is God. *God is the determining factor!* What enabled these people to persevere when being sawed in two is a strong belief that God is better than anything this life can give and better than anything death can take.'

"Go, Piper! Yeah, Piper! That was sweet! Don't mess with Piper 'cause he'll lay the smack down!"

I thought of that hippie Jesus Freak in the *Life* photograph receiving blessing and warmth from that intimate God and could not reconcile that image with jeers, flogging, chains, sheepskins, goatskins, and being put in prison, stoned, and sawed in two. Nor could I relate it to an edgy trembling teen, flat out on the floor of a bus, prostrate before the awesome God who could smash you like an ant. Wasn't God that dreamy presence toward whom I stretch out my arms to receive?

While I wrestled with these seemingly conflicting pictures of God, I also contended with bouts of insomnia caused by hot flashes and "hormonal rage," as a charming, endearing male once put it. I felt I had lost myself *and* God. I wasn't the Jesus Freak in the picture anymore. I wasn't receiving. In fact, I was losing. My sons were hooting from the pews at sermons about being sawed in two and falling prostrate on bus floors because of the God they owned, while I felt as if all my internal support structures were collapsing underneath me.

One night, unable to sleep, I got up and went downstairs to make toast. I was pulling a knife from the silverware drawer to butter it and heard myself utter, "Praying doesn't do any good." I wondered why God made all these promises in the Scriptures about the power of prayer and so on when, lost as I was, it seemed he either did not hear and so attend these prayers or heard and remained unmoved. I didn't understand the God I had owned as a teen. I wanted to understand him the way my sons did. I wanted their exalted vision. I wanted to fall down on the floor of a bus and see his beauty and rest in his sovereignty the way they said they did.

About that time Jon and I had been scheduled to teach junior church. That summer, Jon was in his "Jesus phase." He was growing his hair long and wore a beard and sandals and minimal clothing, stopping just short of obscenity. My brother said he looked like a combination of Bob (my husband), Jesus, and Ronald McDonald, which, in any case, had its endearing effects on the four-to-eight-year-olds we were to teach in junior church. They looked up to him as if he were Jesus himself. We handed out paper and crayons, and Jon told the kids to draw tulips. Then he wrote T-U-L-I-P on the chalkboard and told them to write it on their papers next to their flower tulips. Looking like Jesus and being (in their minds) his earthly presence, the children obeyed enthusiastically and drew tulips and wrote the word *TULIP* on their papers.

"I want to draw two tulips," says Japhy.

"That's righteous," says Jon.

"Can I write it in cursive? How do you do a cursive *T*?" asks Clifford.

"Once you get older, you realize how worthless cursive really is," says Jon.

"Can you connect the *U* to a cursive *L*?"

"You can write cursive any way you want."

"Naw. Cursive is too hard." (Clifford abandons the cursive.)

Jon stands by the chalkboard and introduces the lesson. "*TULIP* is a Christian word, kind of," he says. "*T* stands for 'total depravity.' *Depravity* comes from the root word *deprave*. *In no way is there any goodness in something depraved.* Everybody here is totally depraved, as bad as you can get."

"I need the green. It's my turn with the green." (They were sharing crayons, and there were limited numbers.)

"Mario, give Japhy the green. It's his turn," I interject, as the diplomat.

In addition to "looking like Jesus," Jon is an artist, so he enlivened the lesson with visual aids. He took chalk and went to the chalkboard. "It's like, pretend you are an ugly bug being held over a fire." Jon draws an unhappy spider over flames licking at his pointy legs, with several ugly bugs belly up at the bottom of the flames. At that point, all drawings of tulips are abandoned, clean sheets of paper are dispersed, and more fights break out over the orange, yellow, and brown crayons to draw ugly bugs and licking flames.

"The only thing keeping the bug from burning in the fire is God holding it with his fingers," says Jon. He draws a hand clutching the spider between the thumb and first finger. Hands holding spiders are drawn on all the pictures.

Jon moves on to the *U* of *TULIP:* "Unconditional election," he writes on the board. "Everybody knows what a condition is, right?"

"Like air conditioning?" asks Mario.

"A condition is like when, to get ice cream, you have to eat broccoli."

There are groans. The word *yuck* can be heard.

"Unconditional election means you could eat all the broccoli in the world, but it won't guarantee getting ice cream. God chooses some ugly bugs not to let go of. He keeps them from the fire just because he wants to."

"Was Jesus an ugly bug?"

"No. Jesus was beautiful," Jon says.

The crayon wars calm as the kids innovate using reds and blues for flames. One draws a green bug.

Clifford notes, "Bugs boil up when they go into fires."

Jon concurs and moves on to *L*: "Limited atonement means Jesus died for people who don't burn in hell."

"Jesus died for our sins," says Noey, one of the few girls in the class.

"Jesus didn't die for the bugs being dropped into the fire," says Jon.

Again, as the diplomat, I prod Jon on to the letter *I*.

"Irresistible grace," he says. "If you are God's elect, you want God so bad it's all you want."

"What's *P?*" someone asks (I didn't see who).

"Perseverance of the saints—"

Clifford interrupts: "Like Saint Francis of Assisi?"

"A 'saint' is a Christian. Perseverance means you will never be dropped into the fire." Jon puts down the chalk. "Okay. To review, what saves us?"

"Being good," says Clifford.

"No, you're absolutely wrong! You're totally depraved! You can never be good enough to save yourself!"

"God is in charge," says Mario to a baffled but unruffled Clifford.

"Yes, God is in charge," says Jon.

"I don't go to church that much," says Clifford.

"Going to church doesn't decide whether you're a Christian," says Jon, and Clifford seems comforted. "God is holding you over the pit of hell with his fingers right now."

"What if the bug slips out of his hand on accident?" asks Japhy.

"There are no accidents. God is perfect," says Jon. "Now listen, this is important," Jon says, wrapping up the lesson.

"When you guys fight God, you're fighting the hand that holds you over the fire. When you break free, you drop into the fire. So don't fight God, okay? Hang on tight to God."

"Look at my picture." Clifford shows it to Jon.

"That's awesome. Dang. That's righteous," says Jon.

❄ ❄ ❄

I needed to understand this edgy—they'd call it hard-core—faith of these teens. So over the years I have observed, researched, and studied youth culture to try to get my head around what makes these young people tick. In some small way I have begun to understand why the God they own and worship is more of the ant-smashing disposition than the gentle friend and guide of my hippie Jesus Freak days. Jon wrote a poem a few years ago that captures a glimpse of the state of mind of his peers:

> distorted reflection
> pathetic selection
> insufficiency
> pleasurable efficiency
> blank stare
> headed nowhere
> sexually motivated
> morally castrated
> inattentive
> unrepentant
> downward trend
> poison-stemmed

living in denial
empty smile
unattractive
helplessly inactive
needed anesthetic
completely apathetic
what then can I conclude?
I'm developing a nihilistic attitude.

I have come to see that today's youth culture has a fixation on death. A "nihilistic attitude" reflects a present-day version of the philosophy of Friedrich Nietzsche (1844–1900), who held that to be truly human (his idea of "Superman") is to be liberated from constraints imposed from religion and morality. According to Nietzsche, the true human answers to no one. He went so far as to say, "So that man may respect himself he must be capable of doing evil."

It is sad that casting off moral constraints and, in its most extreme expression, embracing evil, have marked the age we live in. Most high schoolers haven't undertaken a thorough and serious study of Nietzsche (though some have). But his philosophy is widely disseminated in pop culture, and one venue where it is evident, surprisingly, has been on T-shirts.

Ben was a senior in high school when, walking to his car parked off school property, he saw one of his peers from school putting on a T-shirt that said "Christian Killer." Rather than feel threatened, Ben wanted to understand why this kid "wanted to 'kill'" someone like him—or at least why he would advertise the notion on a T-shirt. Ben decided to get to know him. As it turns out, this young man numbered himself among the so-called Goths in the school, a fringe group whose devotees are known by their dark clothing, brooding dispositions, social isolation, and shocking T-shirts. Ben started to sit with the Goths during study hall.

He learned that the Goth subculture, such as it is, has been heavily influenced by Nietzsche's Superman, which, in today's culture, translates into the brooding antihero. Goths embrace the notion that there is no God and so, no moral absolutes and no one to answer to. Each person becomes his or her own god.

Ben also learned through his Goth friends that most had not studied Nietzsche and that their philosophical "expertise" came from a few atheistic Web sites they had visited. Their preoccupation with death and killing and Christian hating arose more from being outcast, damaged, and hurt than from a true philosophical center. Ben discovered that the young man who wore the "Christian Killer" T-shirt did so for the shock value, to get attention. "People paid attention to him if he wore a shirt like that," says Ben.

Death themes also play out in youth culture in positive expressions. Again, one vehicle for the dissemination of such themes has been T-shirts. This past year, before their yearly retreat, my son's youth group held a T-shirt contest, asking kids to design a shirt that would capture the theme for the weekend. My son came up with a shirt that said *Nachfolge* on the front, and on the back it read: "When Christ calls a man, he bids him come and die." *Nachfolge* is the original German title of Dietrich Bonhoeffer's *The Cost of Discipleship*. The quotation on the back comes from that book. That design won the contest. Come and die for Christ became the theme of the youth group retreat.

On another occasion, when Ben was seventeen, he came bounding into my bedroom after youth group and announced that when he died, he wanted us to play the Supertones' song "Heaven" at his memorial service. My blood ran cold. Then I said, "Okay." (What else could I say? No?)

I wondered why death would loom large in the minds of youth and came to see that the answer is obvious. They are the "generation of the school shootings," as one Columbine student once said to me. This and other school shootings have taken away the notion, so typical of the teen mind-set, that they can live forever. The shootings have left young people saying (and I've heard it many times), "We might not be here tomorrow, so we better say what we've got to say now."

But more than being the generation of the shootings, they are the generation of the teen martyrs. Two of the kids who died at Columbine did so making confessions of faith in God. The martyrdoms set the standard for what it means to live for God. They have demonstrated to their peers that God is not only worth living for but worth dying for. This sets them apart from the otherwise appetite-driven, self-serving youth culture that allows each person to define *truth* by his or her individual sensibilities. The martyrdoms demonstrated that God is not another consumer option, which introduces a new possibility to a jaded, cynical, despairing teen culture. It has aroused spiritual sensibilities. And the fact that this faith presumes a cost—maybe death—is part of its force and appeal. Faith, for them, is not a receiving kind of thing, like the picture of the Jesus Freak in the *Life* photo. Faith in God is an urgent, self-surrendering thing that demands one give up everything, maybe even life. For this generation, being a Jesus Freak means being someone who is willing to die for the faith. The recent book *Jesus Freaks,* by dc Talk with The Voice of the Martyrs, highlights martyrdoms throughout church history, up to and including Cassie Bernall's at Columbine High School. It is written for teens and is a best-seller.

※ ※ ※

During that sleepless night, after eating toast and uttering the despairing thought that prayer doesn't do any good, I tossed in my bed while the hands on the clock inched toward 3:00 A.M. That's when I caught a glimpse of what my sons saw when they thought about God. In my head I heard the verse, "Whether we live or die, we belong to the Lord." In that moment, dimly, I saw myself from a different vantage point, not as the emotive disciple in cutoffs with arms outstretched for receiving, but as one inside something bigger than I. It wasn't so much about my "receiving" as about God's *being*, and my fitting into *that*. I saw myself inside something that had boundaries and protection and the feeling that no matter how close I went to the edges, I couldn't cross over and get lost. I couldn't sleep that night because, in a way, I felt as if I were carrying the burden of my calling, as if my purpose, my success and/or failure depended upon what I "received" and so made happen, as if my destiny were in my hands. Not being able to sleep, and therefore function, jeopardized my call, my destiny. When I heard "Whether we live or die, we belong to the Lord," I took rest in the thought that God's presence and my purpose do not stand or fall with me. Whether I sleep or don't sleep, I am the Lord's. Whether I can get up tomorrow or can't, I am the Lord's. My goals and his purpose do not depend upon my ability to get up in the morning. He is the one who orders my successes or failures. Whether I succeed or fail, I am the Lord's.

There is no place to go when you can't sleep except, ultimately, back to bed. The same is true when it comes to understanding God. When you're backed up against a wall, wondering where he is and whether he sees you and hears your cries and you're not sure he's there, the only place to go is back to God. Then things open up. Then there is rest.

This picture of God also helped me understand why death looms large in the minds of these hard-core Christian teens. "Whether [you] live or die, [you] are the Lord's." "Living" and "dying," in other words, are beside the point. This makes these teens the perfect ambassadors to a despairing, nihilistic youth culture that is preoccupied with death. It is why Ben had the courage—and the desire—to get to know the Goth kid wearing the "Christian Killer" T-shirt. When Jon saw a vision of God as the awesome One who could smash him like an ant, he understood how vulnerable we are as mere humans, which awakened his senses to the grace and beauty God bestows day in and day out when he gives life and health and the ability to wake up in the morning and put on our shoes. It's similar to Jon's reply when I asked him if he

thought thirty dollars was fair payment for the girl who
would be watering my flowers when we were away and he said,
"Well, to be fair, she deserves to burn in hell. But, yeah."
The "but yeah" is that well-being. Anything that isn't on par
with burning in hell is more than fair. That way of thinking
changes your outlook.

We are "aliens and strangers on earth . . . longing for a
better country—a heavenly one," as John Piper noted in the
text from his smack-down sermon. Which means, essentially,
that it doesn't really matter so much whether we live or die.
The point is that we are the Lord's. True Jesus Freaks get
that. They are the ones who are willing to die for their faith
because, in a way, they have already lost their lives.

I hope I have helped my sons see that God can also be a
warm healer and friend. But they have helped me understand his bigness in a way I hadn't before. Still, they are my
sons and typical teens. On Jon's bookshelf, next to his copies
of Nietszche, Bonhoeffer, Lewis, and Piper, is a copy of Jack
Handey's *Deeper Thoughts* ("Whenever someone asks me to
define love, I usually think for a minute, then I spin around
and pin the guy's arm behind his back. *Now* who's asking the
questions?"). He dyed his hair blue for school pictures his
junior year (though, admittedly, when he did so, we were
having a discussion about John Wesley's theology of Christian perfection). And not too long ago Ben told me that in
the body of Christ, he and Jon are the fists.

This elicited on my part a need for further elucidation.

Their spiritual gift is "fighting," he said, and he cited
Proverbs 20:30 as their text: "Blows and wounds cleanse

away evil, and beatings purge the inmost being." They fight
to encourage people; it's a means of fellowship, he says. They
don't pick fights in the bullying sense, but they sponsor
"Fight Nights," where they invite their like-minded fist-
gifted believing friends and also unbelieving friends to come
and watch while, two at a time, they do all sorts of nasty
things to one another until one, the loser, "taps out." The
visitors love it. It allows the teens' unbelieving friends to
"have fun" in the context of "Christian fellowship" and is a
way of introducing them to Christ. When the fighting is
over, ice packs on eyes and shoulders, the guys share the
gospel and talk about what it means to belong to Christ. In
the movie *Fight Club,* Ben says, "the fighting is like a catharsis;
you know, like how in Buddhism you meditate to empty
yourself. In Christianity, we transform it. We celebrate it.
We love fighting. We do it with all our hearts. It's encourage-
ment through physical punishment." He then cites Piper:
"God is most glorified in us when we are most satisfied
in him." (And I am left to wonder whether John Piper
envisioned fighting as the vehicle of such satisfaction and
glory.) Unlike the one of the hippie in cutoffs with splayed
palms, bruised eyes and rug burns seem an apt picture for
understanding what it means to be a Jesus Freak in today's
world.

And so, I face one of life's hard passages. I've buried my
father. I've moved my mother into a retirement community.
I've packed two of my three children off to college. I'm looking at my last year with my final child at home. I'm thinking
about opportunities missed, and regrets, and dreams that

aren't going to come true on this side of eternity. I'm not sleeping well. I look in the mirror and don't know who I'm looking at. Is God in this picture?

My sons have helped me answer that question. They've shown me that God's movement doesn't depend upon the measure of my faith or on my inclinations to "receive." They have helped me see that whether I am saved by my faith and am enabled to endure suffering because of that faith, *God is the determining factor!* Whether I sleep or don't sleep, whether I live or die, I am the Lord's, and fighting him means fighting the hand that holds me over the fire. Jesus Freaks stand in the strong belief that God is better than anything this life can give and better than anything death can take. They have packed their bags for heaven. That is why Ben told me what song he wanted sung at his memorial service. It is why they say what they've got to say now. It is why I am asking myself if I am still a Jesus Freak.

12 *Coach*

Our lives are sacred journeys along rocky paths, and sometimes we travel with stones in our shoes. There is a way
forward. I found it in a surprising place. I saw it when a
young boy said to my son Jon during his eighth-grade year,
"Your mom cries all the time, doesn't she?"

We were attending an all-day tournament for IKWF
(Illinois Kids Wrestling Federation) when that boy made his
observation. The truth is, I don't cry all the time. But I cry
at my son's wrestling meets. So I understand why that young
man thought I did.

Columnist Susan Brimer of the *Chicago Sun-Times*
recounted the advice her husband gave their son when he
announced he was going out for high school wrestling. "They
talk about playing soccer or playing baseball, even playing
football. But nobody talks about 'playing' wrestling, and
there is a reason for that. It is a combat sport." Two of my
sons took up the same challenge, which, to some degree,

explains why I am reduced to raw emotion when they step
onto the wrestling mat. (There is a reason mothers are
prohibited from accompanying their sons when they join the
armed forces.)

At first, my bizarre show of emotion shocked and
confounded me. I am embarrassed to think that the year of
the IKWF sectional when Jon was in eighth grade, his coach's
sustaining image of me is of an eye-bulging, vein-popping
lunatic hovering on the edge of the ridiculous.

Wrestling's combat motif alone did not explain the
weeping. I know this because it started early in the season
when I was sitting in the bleachers by myself watching the
wrestlers come and go before and after their bouts. Win
or lose, after the match the first thing they did was to go
to the opposing coach to shake his hand. The second
thing they did was to return to their coach, our coach,
Coach John. Coach would do what I was to learn he always
did with every kid after every match, win or lose. Whether
it was the scrappy sinewy lightweight wrestler who couldn't
be pinned or taken down or the lumbering heavyweight
who could barely control his own momentum, after each
match Coach cupped their faces in both hands, looked
them in the eye, and talked to them till their vision
cleared and their chins were erect. Win or lose, those
wrestlers walked off the mat with a steady gate and their
heads up. More than once that year I found myself sitting
in the bleachers midseason—when nothing was at stake—
reduced to tears *between matches* as I watched Coach talk life
back into his wrestlers.

✳ ✳ ✳

You have to understand the wrestling subculture in order to
appreciate the emotive force of this so-called sport. My
indoctrination took place in small steps when two of my sons
were in junior high school. It takes time to figure out what is
happening on the mat, when points—matches even—are won
or lost by the slightest of bodily movements. In any case, all
parents are instantly baptized the first time their child steps
onto the mat. No one prepares you for that moment. There
is no preparing for it. On the day of my initiation I ambled
into the gym, smiling and waving at other moms, recognizing
one or two from the previous spring season when our sons
played Little League baseball together. I looked for my sons'
team colors—black and yellow—and nestled my way into a seat
in the bleachers. I found my sons and waved. Only one saw
me. He lifted his chin. He did not wave.

At the time, the 103 weight class was wrestling—skinny
little guys that looked as if they could be blown over with a
gentle, lapping sea breeze. I watched them and thought, *Wow,
I didn't know little guys like that could have muscle tone.* In due course I
saw my son stand up. He was jumping slightly and rolling
his head about to loosen his neck. He pulled off his sweat-
shirt and sweatpants. This was the first time I saw him in
his "singlet," a wrestling uniform that looks like an old-
fashioned bathing suit some guy might have worn in the 1930s.

I hadn't noticed before how skinny his legs looked, or his
knocked knees. I could have sworn his arm muscles were
bigger than that. Anyway, he was dancing around, shaking his

arms, jogging in place. A fellow wrestler took his hands and jostled his arms in waving motions, up and down. *Why all this ritual?* I wondered. Several minutes passed before the 103s finished their match. The little guy on our team stood in the center of the circle on the mat. The referee raised his arm. He won. That's nice. Way to go, peanut.

Young wrestlers with ever increasing heights, weights, and buff quotients continued the ritual cycle of loosening, then wrangling with the opponent. They bent toward one another, locked heads, grabbed shoulder blades, twisted each other's backs, drove their heads into each other's sides, sprawled spread-eagle, grunted, heaved, and sweat. Then—ouch—what was that? A takedown. A takedown is good for the person who ends up on top. Two points. Control.

Admittedly, I felt a twinge of compassion for the boy on the bottom. I didn't care if he was on the other team. Couldn't they be a little nicer about it? I checked my watch, still waiting for my son's first time on the mat. I started thinking about what to make for dinner. I had forgotten to take something out of the freezer. What can I make that doesn't require something being taken out of the freezer?

I saw my son step up to the scorer's table to check in. Every wrestler, I was to learn, must do this before every match. He was wearing that old-fashioned bathing suit and, now, head-gear. I smiled and waved. He didn't see me. He was not looking at me. He was not looking at anyone or anything. He was "focused."

The contenders on the mat had just finished their bout. The other team's wrestler won that one. He stood in the

circle and the ref raised his arm. My son was bouncing up
and down on the sidelines. The dog-tired wrestlers who'd
just completed their bout walked off the mat. My son walked
on. Then something started to happen inside my stomach. I
groaned. I began to breathe heavily.

My son was facing the other wrestler, a mirror image of
himself, more or less—same height, same weight—their hands
raised, palms open, fingers curled like they were ready to
tear each other's heads off. My heart started to race. I was
sweating. My face and neck got hot. I felt nauseated. I wanted
to say, "Wait a minute" to someone. But to whom? The
other moms in the bleachers were checking their watches,
wondering what to cook for dinner. My son was either about
to shoot against and crush his opponent or be shot against
and crushed by him. The shooting and crushing would
continue for three periods; one minute-long period and two
minute-and-a-half periods. (They are longer in high school
wrestling.) *What kind of sport is this?*

By the end of that four-minute match, my son's first, and
so my rite of initiation into the Tribe of Wrestling Parents,
my veins were bulging, my head was throbbing from the
blood that had rushed into it from all the screaming, my eyes
were wet from the sobbing, my face was flushed, and I had
almost wet my pants.

As I said, every parent is initiated the first time their child
steps onto the mat. I heard one mother let out a blood-
curdling, earsplitting scream after her son pulled out a
particularly grueling, gut-wrenching victory at the end of
his match. I could relate.

Fully ensconced as a member of the tribe, I came to feel at home in our "temple," the gym, a cavernous maw of human smells and mildewing gym shoes, dimly lit by fluorescent bulbs that made the wounded and exhausted look like the living dead. It became our second home. Its accoutrements were part of our everyday life. Things like the throw-up bucket on the edge of every mat, used by wrestlers at any point in any match. The wads of cotton ready to be stuffed in their noses when the bleeding starts. The ice packs, also ready to go, for when a shoulder separates or a knee is hyperextended or a neck gets wrenched when a wrestler lands headfirst. Wrestling parents in-the-know keep a steady supply of Lamisil. Experience has shown it to be the best antifungal cream for knocking out ringworm, which is part of everyday life for a wrestler. It is part of the vocabulary, like *Bible study* is to a born-again Christian. Keeping a steady supply of anti-inflammatories, we discovered, also helped.

School wrestling meets were on weekdays. But it was the all-day weekend tournaments, of which there were many, that tested the mettle of the wrestler and his parents. They must arrive before dawn to weigh in, frequently after wrestling the previous night in the school league. The actual wrestling begins several hours later and can easily last until well past six in the evening. You arrive when it's dark and return home when it's dark, spending the day in the temple of the living dead. Between bouts, fathers read newspapers, do crossword puzzles, or calculate seeding brackets, while mothers push Gatorade and power bars into the faces of their heaving, sweating, bloodied offspring. Some knit. During the matches themselves, mothers have been known to scream, shake their fists, jump up and down, and sometimes collapse and beat the mat—or, in my case, sob. Fathers lean on the edge of the bleachers, bat newspapers, and bellow monosyllabic instructions. *Shoot! Dig! Fight! Pin!*

This is the solidarity of the tribe.

The glue that holds us all together—the sobbing, screaming mothers, the barking, bellowing fathers, the writhing, grunting competitors on the mat—is Coach.

❊ ❊ ❊

I asked Jon one time if he could hear me yelling to him from the side of the mat.

He said no. "The only voice I hear is Coach's."

Coach John would sit in his chair on the corner of the mat, elbows on his knees, hands curled around his mouth. He would be telling Jon when to shoot, when to lift his head or keep it down, which leg to rotate, how much time is left, when to stand, when to breathe.

The IKWF sectional was the climactic tournament of Jon's eighth-grade season. It would determine who went to State, the ultimate prize. The middle school our sons attended was one of the smaller ones in our town, and the wrestling program was not a priority. Coach John came in, took this ragtag group of Hulk Hogan wanna-bes (most young people wrongly associate real wrestling with its banal WWF impostor) and made real wrestlers out of them. They came through the regular season grabbing second place in the division conference. At the IKWF stage, wrestlers competed on an individual basis for advancement to state competition.

The morning of the sectional we arrived predawn, as usual. The wrestling hadn't started. Coach sat Jon down with the seeding chart. We looked over their shoulders. Then he walked Jon through the brackets. "Okay," he said, "you beat this guy—" pointing to Jon's first opponent in the lower brackets—"then you'll wrestle one of these two—" pointing to higher seeds. "Probably him." He points. "You lost to him once, but you can beat him."

I am listening to this thinking, I have seen my son come away from matches with broken blood vessels dotting his face, blood dripping from his nose and mouth (braces are hard on wrestlers), his neck wrenched so that he couldn't straighten it, his eyes swollen, his face and arms and shoulders streaked with mat burns. I am stalled at the "you beat this guy" part of Coach's seeding strategy. Coach said things like that all the time, as if it were mathematical.

When, as predicted, Jon won his first match, Coach was neither surprised nor elated. He rubbed Jon's neck after the match, explained how his opponent got that escape, and demonstrated with bodily movements the way Jon could've turned him on his back for the pin.

In preparation for the second match, I rubbed Jon's back and gave him an anti-inflammatory. He was battling a twisted neck that prevented him from rotating his head. Plus, his shoulder hurt. Bad rotator cuffs run in our family. He tried to rest, lying flat on the bleacher between matches. An hour after his first match his weight class was called to mat number two.

Coach loosened his arms with that jiggling, waving thing. He rubbed Jon's neck on the spot where it hurt. Jon stepped onto the mat, and Coach took his seat in the corner. My husband and I were on the floor at the edge of the mat. The sobbing usually didn't start until about the second period.

Coach called out the shoots, pivots, foot placement, head placement. He told Jon where to be for the starting position after time had been called or between periods. Sometimes "up," sometimes "down," sometimes "neutral." I never understood the strategy behind this. Between periods, as Jon labored for air, hands on knees, bleeding at the mouth, unable to raise his arm above his head because of the rotator problem, Coach talked him back onto the mat. Had I been Jon, I would have crawled through the sewer first.

Jon lost the second match. Coach said, "We'll come back and wrestle for third."

The problem with this scenario that particular day, however, was that "wrestling for third" (and so a trip to State) meant taking on a well-sculpted pretty boy in need of an attitude adjustment. He came into that match with a 31-and-1 record. He annoyed me.

I don't remember much about the match. I was sobbing in the first period, I remember that. I couldn't hear what Coach was telling Jon to do. I don't remember what my husband and I were yelling from the sidelines. I do remember my husband pulling me back once. Was I crawling onto the mat? Unbelievably, Jon beat this guy 7 to 2. The ref raised my son's aching arm, and the pretty boy, now 31 and 2, walked off the mat crying.

It was late in the afternoon by the time Jon's fourth and final match rolled around, the match that would confer or deny state contention. Both wrestlers were scraping to the bone by this point. Coach's voice was hoarse. My head ached.

The contenders lumbered onto the mat, shook hands, and threw their weary arms toward one another in sluggish, laboring motions. Every second on the time clock felt like three. The combatants grunted, moved slowly, achingly. This match wasn't about shooting and finessing. It was about digging into negative territory to summon strength that wasn't there. Neither wrestler scored any points during the first period. They pressed on. Now and then one might rally and exert a flourish of strength against the other, who in turn would summon something from somewhere to respond. No points were scored the second period. The score was 0 to 0 going into the final two minutes.

Coach came up with a strategy. The opponent chose "down" for the starting position at the beginning of the third period, meaning he would start on all fours and Jon would be over him, holding him around the waist in a position of dominance. Coach John's thinking went this way: Jon is "up"—fine—the whistle blows, which starts the clock, and Jon releases the guy. Granted, that gives his opponent a free point for an escape, but, Coach's strategy went, Jon's strong suit was takedowns, which are worth two points. So Jon releases the guy, which sets him up for the takedown, and then Jon gets the takedown and wins the match, 2 to 1.

The buzzer sounded, marking the start of period three. Executing Coach's plan, Jon released his opponent, who stood up unchallenged. The ref raised his arm, signaling one point for the opponent. The score was 0 to 1, in favor of the other guy. Jon summoned his strength, heaving, grunting, battling, clawing for the takedown. Then the clock ran out.

In the fog of the moments that followed that defeat, people came up to Jon and told him he wrestled with "heart." Jon's opponent, to whom Jon had freely rendered the ticket to State, put his hand on Jon's shoulder and said, "You should be the one going to State, not me."

❄ ❄ ❄

Whether Jon should or shouldn't have been the one to go to State, I can't say, though I agree that my son wrestled with heart. Wrestling isn't like other sports. You don't "play" wrestling. It is hand-to-hand combat. It is you and the other guy with no place to hide. And Coach.

Seeing him in the corner helped me understand something I have never forgotten, and it explains the weeping. There is something almost mystical about what this sport pulls out of a person. There is something about battling through a match till you scrape to the bone and then feeling the arms of your coach, the one who holds your face, clears your eyes, and sets you walking straight again, that is essential to our humanness. Coach is the one who got you ready for the match, who put you there, and then got you through it. It's devotional. Sometimes that kind of devotion gets you to State. Sometimes it doesn't. But getting through the eighth-grade wrestling season with our son Jon and battling through that IKWF sectional showed me that State, when it came to

this so-called sport, was beside the point. Where does the
strength come from to keep going out onto the mat? From
where does the trust arise that enables you to execute a move
that helps your opponent? How do you learn how to believe
like that? To submit your judgment to someone else's even
when logic dictates against it? How do you get to a place
where your heart, your mind, your body have found har-
mony in submission to someone else?

There is nowhere to hide when you're on that mat, no
place to go except straight through three periods of combat.
There is a cacophony of other voices yelling instructions
from the sidelines. But only one voice knows your strengths,
your weak spots, your endurance level, where your neck
hurts. Wrestling with Coach John was a lesson in discipleship
for our son. He learned how to follow, hear, trust, obey, and
lay it all on the line—and lose. It enlarged my son's soul.

That's why I cry at wrestling meets. I cry all the time.
Coach with his wrestlers is the picture of devotion in battle.
It is the picture of a good shepherd who knows his sheep,
who leads his sheep, and whose sheep hear his voice and
listen to that voice.

That's what our son Jon took away from that harrowing
day at the IKWF sectionals when, because of a freely surrendered point, he did not advance to State. That drama plays
out again and again on the wrestling mat, and in the human
heart. It is playing out right now, inside me. It's what keeps
me moving forward on the rocky path of this sacred journey,
even when there are stones in my shoes.

Jon was ready to go home. He couldn't wait to dig into an

unopened bag of DoubleStuf Oreo cookies waiting for him, a treat he had been denied for three grueling months of cutting weight. We gathered our coats, water bottles, newspaper, empty Gatorade bottles, and well-worn bracket booklet, and packed it in for another season. We wanted to find Coach John before we left. Jon's middle-school wrestling career was over. He'd be moving to the high school level, with longer, more grueling matches against bigger, meaner, nastier, head-twisting opponents. He'd be moving on without Coach John. We wanted to thank him and say good-bye. We felt bonded to him. We wondered how Jon would get through the rest of his wrestling career without him.

We didn't get the chance to say these things. Coach was sitting in another wrestler's corner. He was telling him when to shoot, when to drive, when to lift his head, when to sprawl. He was talking life into that wrestler, telling him he could beat this guy.

Conclusion

I remember as a young Christian having a day when I felt depressed. I mentioned it to an older woman at the church I was attending, who was all smiles and had shining eyes. She said, "Just praise the Lord." I looked at her, not knowing how to respond. "Just praise him!" she reiterated. I wondered what was wrong with me that left such a gap between my reality and that prescription for wholeness.

It turned out that "just praising him" didn't satisfy even this woman's tormented heart. She ended up leaving the church a few years after that conversation. Behind the smiles and bright eyes was a woman struggling with pain and contradictions that resulted in an illicit relationship with another member of that church. Many were shocked, as I was. But at the same time I have thought many times since—*I am not surprised*. It is easy to dismiss authentic human distress and exchange it for platitudes and formulaic prescriptions for getting on in the Christian life. We do so to our detriment as human beings and to the dishonoring of the name of Jesus, who died for lost people, people like you and me.

In contrast to that, also early in my Christian walk, I grabbed onto another piece of sage advice that has had staying power. It came from Billy Graham—bless that man—who was speaking at that evangelism praisefest I attended sponsored by Campus Crusade for Christ: Explo '72. He said, "It is not easy to be a New Testament Christian." It was the first time I felt someone was being honest with me about what this was all about. I don't condemn those who, back then, touted only praise, joy, peace—all that—as the defining features of the Christian life. But Billy Graham's statement helped me understand that while praise, joy, and peace are God-centered ideals, the real world has a way of messing things up and keeping our heavenly wings pinned to earth. He helped me reckon with the reality that sometimes there is no peace and that joy is somewhere else, not here.

We walk on. Whether in joy or sorrow, in praise or lament, in peace or tumult, the road leads us forward, and we must keep walking, even when it hurts. I have said that sometimes it feels as if there are stones in our shoes. But if we walk, in time we reach a place where we look back. That's when we see that all along, God was leading us, though we didn't know it or feel it or praise him for it.

As one of four young girls growing up in an alcoholic home, I didn't see God's careful eye watching over us during those dark years. But it was. I didn't quite get it when my grandmother scribbled out that dependent clause so many years ago. But now I understand that that was a signal God gave me to help me believe I had something to give. My niece Kelly died, and our world fell apart. But the sun kept coming up, and the lawn needed mowing. We had to figure a way to get through it. God met us there, too, sister with sister, a sacred mystical bond. Church life is no less complicated than everyday real life and, in some ways, more so. I still wonder sometimes what the Lord Jesus was thinking when he deigned this institution, the church, to be his "bride." We are a blemished bride at best. But that is the beauty of it, I reckon. God ekes out holiness in spite of ourselves. Life's choices come and go, like the choice my husband made to give up that church so I could realize my dream. Sometimes you wonder what might have happened if you had done it some other way. You learn painfully that there is life in sacrificing your will to someone else's, and sometimes there is death. We move along the road less traveled, and God somehow conforms our choices into his plan. He sometimes gives visions, as he did to my grandmother and my father. But what then? People think you're crazy in the telling. Is there no easy way? No, really, there isn't. But whether we live or die, we are the Lord's. He is the one who will carry us through. I think of Coach John, sitting in the corner of the wrestling mat, pouring his life and strength into the faltering wills of his wrestlers. That picture helps me keep putting one foot in front of the other. There are so many other voices clamoring to pull us off our course. But only one Voice speaks life into us and can carry us through to the end. Do you hear it? He is speaking to you, right now, even as he is speaking to me.

Sources

✦

Introduction

Chapter 1: A Sword through Her Soul

14: "forced [him]": Luke 23:26

14: "Dear woman": John 19:26, NIV

14: "Here is": John 19:26, NIV

14: "Here is": John 19:27, NIV

15: "Who is": Matthew 12:48

Chapter 2: Sisters' Reunion

29: "Jesus was": N. T. Wright, *The Lord and His Prayer* (Grand Rapids: Eerdmans, 1997), 69.

Chapter 3: Eternity Backwards

38: "her eager student": Gordon Sander, *Serling, the Rise and Twilight of Television's Last Angry Man* (New York: Dutton, 1992), 59.

49: "cloud of witnesses": Hebrews 12:1, NIV

49: "I want you": Fyodor Dostoyevsky, *The Brothers Karamazov*, trans. Andrew R. MacAndrew (New York: Bantam Books, 1970), 934.

Chapter 4: Kelly's Gift

57: "One thing I ask": Psalm 27:4, NIV

57: "He will keep": Psalm 27:5, NIV

61: "He has broken": Lamentations 3:16-24, NIV

61: "Let the little": Matthew 19:14, NIV

66: "I will be glad": Psalm 31:7-9, 14-16, NIV

68: "Sir, come down": John 4:49, NIV

Chapter 5: This Is My Body

86: "who were contributing": Luke 8:3

86: "You Philippians": Philippians 4:15

86: "They sold": Acts 2:45

86: "go and make": Matthew 28:19-20

93: "Daughter,": Mark 5:34

93: "something to eat": See Luke 8:54-55

95: "Listen to my prayer": Psalm 55:1-2, 4-7, NIV

Chapter 6: Pop's Garden

104: "How can": John 14:5-6

104: "To the thirsty": Revelation 21:6-7, RSV

105: "Behold": Isaiah 25:9, NKJV

105: "He who conquers": Revelation 21:7, RSV

Chapter 8: The Harvest

124: "'When my heart": Psalm 61:2, NKJV

Chapter 9: The Road Less Traveled

134: "submit": Ephesians 5:22

134: "Love your": Ephesians 5:25

136: "the evidence": Hebrews 11:1

140: "Two roads diverged": Robert Frost, "The Road Not Taken"

142: "is costly": Dietrich Bonhoeffer, *The Cost of Discipleship* (New York: Macmillan, 1963), 47.

143: "Every moment": Fyodor Dostoyevsky, *The Brothers Karamazov*, trans. Andrew R. MacAndrew (New York: Bantam, 1970), 439.

143: "The way": Bonhoeffer, *The Cost of Discipleship*, 211–212.

143: "If we behold": Bonhoeffer, *The Cost of Discipleship*, 212.

144: "A true act": Dostoyevsky, *The Brothers Karamazov*, 66–67.

145: "To dream": Jim Elliot, *Shadow of the Almighty* (Grand Rapids: Zondervan, 1958), 191.

145: "Faith": Oswald Chambers, *My Utmost for His Highest* (New York: Dodd, Mead, 1935), 305.

145: "You are": Psalm 119:57, NIV

146: "Don't rejoice": Luke 10:20

Chapter 10: Visions

157: "I shall be": Psalm 17:15, KJV

157: "The night": Romans 13:12, KJV

157: "He shall be": 2 Samuel 23:4, KJV

163: "O Sovereign Lord": Ezekiel 20:49

163: "Son of man": Ezekiel 21:2

163: "Son of man": Ezekiel 21:6

163: "Son of man": Ezekiel 21:9

163: "Son of man": Ezekiel 21:12

163: "Son of man": Ezekiel 21:14

163: "Son of man": Ezekiel 21:19

163: "The Lord took": Ezekiel 37:1-4, 9

166: "They are": Ezekiel 20:49

Chapter 11: Jesus Freaks

172: "Some faced": Hebrews 11:36-38, NIV

177: "distorted reflection": copyright 2000 by Jon Zoba

178: "So that man": Friedrich Nietzsche, *The Will to Power*, trans. Walter Kaufman (New York, Random House, 1969), 163.

179: "When Christ calls": Dietrich Bonhoeffer, *The Cost of Discipleship* (New York: Macmillan, 1963), 99.

181: "Whether we live": Romans 14:8, NIV

183: "aliens": Hebrews 11:13, 16, NIV

183: "Blows": Proverbs 20:30, NIV

About the Author

✢

Wendy Murray Zoba is a seasoned journalist whose writing has been widely published. She has interviewed state leaders, rock stars, Ivy League scholars, street people, and organizers of the Ladies Aid Society—all with an eye for the story. "Every person has a story," she says, "and every story is a testament about God." She lived in Honduras, Central America, for several years, where she was confronted by the despair and hopelessness that can overshadow the lives of the world's poor. This enlarged her heart both as a person and as a writer and quickened her sense of responsibility as a citizen of the richest country on the planet. Her writing conveys all of these passions.

Wendy earned a bachelor of arts degree in religion from Hiram College and a master of arts in theological studies in New Testament from Gordon-Conwell Theological Seminary. She served as a regional reporter for *Time* magazine during her time in Honduras and has worked for more than seven years for *Christianity Today* magazine, first as associate editor and more recently as senior writer. Wendy is the author of *Generation 2K: What Parents and Others Need to Know about the Millennials, Day of Reckoning: Columbine and the Search for America's Soul,* and, with J. I. Packer, *J. I. Packer Answers Questions for Today.*

Wendy and her husband, Robert, a pastor, have three sons, Nate, Ben, and Jon. All three, she says, have grown into gifted young men and, each in his own way, has helped her forge her literary vision. When she's not sitting at her laptop writing or traveling somewhere on assignment, she enjoys spending time on the patio she and her family built. There she listens to the water pouring from one pot to the next in her Mexican fountain, trims Jon's bonsai trees, reposes in the hammock, watches the sunlight glinting through the trees, and looks at the remains of the tree-house her sons built in their younger days. She can think of only one dream she hasn't realized: singing backup for James Taylor or the Dixie Chicks. Even so, she has decided that her patio is as close to heaven as she can get on this side of eternity.